M000023204

Meet Messiah

A Simple Man's Commentary on John

PAUL MURRAY

ISBN 978-1-64191-477-2 (paperback)
ISBN 978-1-64191-478-9 (digital)

Copyright © 2018 by Paul Murray

All rights reserved. No part of this publication may be reproduced, distributed, or transmitted in any form or by any means, including photocopying, recording, or other electronic or mechanical methods without the prior written permission of the publisher. For permission requests, solicit the publisher via the address below.

Christian Faith Publishing, Inc.
832 Park Avenue
Meadville, PA 16335
www.christianfaithpublishing.com

Printed in the United States of America

Contents

Part I

Behold! The Man

Introduction

Steak, Not Milk

For a long time, I have thought that the Gospel of John doesn't get a fair shake by most Christians. Many have the mentality that if you are a new Christian or are thinking about becoming a Christian, John is the place to start reading your Bible. The assumption is that John is easy to read and understand, giving the impression that the content of the gospel is milk and not meat.

In my opinion, the Gospel of John is a twenty-four-ounce porterhouse steak, the kind they serve at Wolf Creek Lodge in Coeur d'Alene, Idaho. Real meat, thick and juicy, cooked to perfection, more than enough to fill the hungriest man. However, to change the analogy just a bit, when prospecting, you have to dig a bit to find the real nuggets. That's what I want to do in this study, dig a bit and find the meat beneath the milk. (Yuk! That's not a good picture!) But here's the real trick. As in my first book, *Pagans, Prostitutes and other Problems*, I want to keep this simple. Folks like me need to be able to understand what is being said and how it is relevant to their lives.

So, let's consider the Gospel of John. One of the obvious questions many people ask is, "Why do we need four gospels? Don't you think one would be enough?" Why didn't these four gospel writers (Matthew, Mark, Luke, and John) just get together and write one big all-inclusive gospel that covered all the events recorded in all four of the gospels? That would make much more sense. In fact, they could have put it all in chronological order and avoided a lot of confusion and seeming conflict between the gospels.

You have to admit, that makes a lot of sense. There are, however, several reasons for the four gospels. One is that according to Jewish law, a matter is established on the basis of two or three eye witnesses.[1]

Here among the four gospel writers we have two direct eye-witness accounts with the writings of both Mathew and John, both apostles. With the addition of the other two gospel writers, Mark and Luke, I would say that the facts have been established with a fine point put on them.

Different Approaches

Another reason for the four gospels is that each writer addresses a different audience with a different purpose. I realize that there is still an on-going debate about "authorship" and "dates" when it comes to the gospel writers, but let's keep it simple.

Matthew wrote his gospel to a Jewish audience, showing that Jesus was the promised King of the Jews. Matthew, also called Levi, was the son of Alpheus[2] and has far more references to the Old Testament than any of the other gospels and Matthew writes with a unique Jewish flavor.

For example, Matthew uses the distinctly Jewish term "kingdom of heaven," where the other books in the New Testament speak only of the "kingdom of God." Only in Matthew does Jesus say, "I was sent only to the lost sheep of the house of Israel." In Matthew, Jesus instructed His disciples "Do not go in the way of the Gentiles, and do not enter any city of the Samaritans, but rather go to the lost sheep of the house of Israel." In Matthew's gospel we find the use of the term *son of David* more times than in all three of the other gospels combined.

---

[1]   Deut. 17:6, 2 Cor. 13:1
[2]   Mark 2:14, Luke 5:27

Matthew records the birth of Jesus because the birth of a King is extremely important. And Matthew traces the genealogy of Jesus from Abraham down through Joseph, demonstrating His right to the throne of David. Jesus is the King of kings, the One whom Matthew declares, in 28:18, has been given all authority in heaven and on earth.

Mark (also known as John Mark[3]) wrote to Gentile readers and a Roman audience in particular. His gospel has a far more fast-paced narrative than the others do. He doesn't present Jesus as a ruler, but as the servant of all. He presents Jesus as the One who ceaselessly seeks and serves those who are lost, as the One willing to give His life as a ransom for many. Mark 10:25 is the key verse of Mark's gospel, "*The Son of Man did not come to be served, but to serve, and to give His life as a ransom for many.*" Mark paints a picture of Jesus as a servant. There is no genealogy in Mark's gospel because there is no concern about the birth or heritage of a servant.

Luke (also the author of the book of Acts) wrote his gospel to a Greek audience. Luke is a doctor and writes to portray Jesus as God's representative man, as God intended man to be. It is Luke who traces Jesus's genealogy from Jesus all the way back to Adam. We all find our common identity as "sons of Adam." Luke's genealogy traces His lineage through Mary and not Joseph, also proving Jesus's right to the throne of David. Luke paints a picture of Jesus as "representative man." Luke does record the birth of Jesus because a man's birth and heritage are important.

So, let's begin with the obvious. Who wrote the book of John? John, of course. But which John? There are several. Was it John Mark? John the Baptist? John the brother of James? John the elder? Which John?

When I started my adult Sunday school class in John, I posed that question. I was surprised at some of the answers. Some thought the author was John the Baptist. I hate to admit this, but two of my

---

[3] Acts 12:12, 25; 15:37

children, who are very bright and mature, thought it was John the Baptist. When they said that, I went into a depression for about three months. How could I have failed so miserably?

It is almost universally understood that John the Apostle, the son of Zebedee,[4] the younger brother of James, was the one who wrote the book of John. However, the evidence to that fact is circumstantial. John doesn't directly address his gospel as Paul does his letters or Peter does his. John never refers to himself directly by name in the book. He can be identified by the expressions *"the disciple whom Jesus loved"* (21:20, 24) and *"the other disciple"* (13:23–24).

Most Unique

Of the four gospels, it is my opinion that John's is the most unique and special for one simple reason. Let me approach that reason through the back door.

Who wrote the book of Matthew? Matthew, of course! And who was Matthew? He was a Jew who had consented to collect taxes from the Jews for the Romans. Because of that, he was hated by orthodox Jews. But Matthew responded to the call of Jesus to *"come and follow me."* He left his job and everything behind to follow Jesus.

Matthew was chosen by Jesus as one of the twelve apostles. He spent the next three years as a faithful follower and disciple. He was an *eyewitness* to the events of which he wrote.

Who wrote the book of Mark? Mark, of course! And who was Mark? He was John Mark, the son of Mary, a woman of wealth and position in Jerusalem (Acts 12:12). Barnabas was his cousin (Col. 4:10). He was a close friend of Peter and mòst likely a convert of the Apostle Peter (1 Pet. 5:13).

Mark accompanied Paul and Barnabas on their first missionary journey, but got homesick and abandoned the journey one-third of the way through. On Paul and Barnabas's second missionary journey,

---

[4]   Matthew 4:21

Barnabas desired to take Mark along again. Paul objected and would have nothing to do with it since Mark had failed them the first time.

A huge disagreement ensued,[5] and Paul and Barnabas wound up parting company. Paul chose Silas as his partner for the second missionary journey and headed off to Asia Minor.[6] Barnabas took Mark and retraced their first journey in an attempt to encourage the churches they had already planted.[7] Much later, Paul reconciled with Mark. In the final days of Paul's life in prison, Mark was one of the few that Paul requested to be with him.[8] Mark was not an eyewitness to the events he wrote. He gained his information from Barnabas, Peter, and Paul.

Who wrote the book of Luke? You're right, Luke. Who was Luke? Luke was the "beloved physician" (Col. 4:14) and a close companion of the Apostle Paul. He is perhaps the only gentile author of any part of the New Testament. We first find Luke hooking up with Paul in Troas, halfway through his second missionary journey in Acts 16, when Paul got the vision to "come to Macedonia."

Luke spent most of the rest of his life with Paul, attending to his needs. He was with him at his death in the Roman dungeon. Luke admits in Luke 1:2 that he was not an eyewitness of the events he records. He probably got most of his information from the Apostle Paul himself.

These first three gospels are call the synoptic gospels. The word *synoptic* means "to see together." They are call *synoptic* because they cover a lot of the same material; they just come at it from different perspectives.

John's gospel is genuinely unique. First of all, John, like Matthew, writes from a personal, *eyewitness* account. He was there. John was the younger brother of James, one of the two sons of thun-

---

[5] Acts 15:36–41
[6] Acts 15:40
[7] Acts 15:39
[8] 2 Tim. 4:11

der. But most uniquely, John was part of Jesus's "inner circle," which consisted of Peter, James, and John.

Yes, Jesus had His favorites. I have my favorites among my four children too. It's just that the position of who is the favorite changes several times a week. Only these three were invited to witness the transfiguration event when Jesus pulled back His humanity and allowed them to see some of his divine glory.[9] Only Peter, James, and John were allowed in with Jesus when He brought back to life the daughter of the synagogue official Jairus.[10] These three also went alone with Jesus up on a mountain to pray.[11] At the Last Supper, when Peter wanted to know who the betrayer was, he asked John, who was reclining on Jesus's breast,[12] to ask Jesus.

John wasn't just an apostle and faithful disciple among the twelve. He was a close personal friend of Jesus. John was the only disciple at the foot of the cross, comforting Jesus's mother during that tragic event. Knowing He was dying, it was John to whom Jesus entrusted the care of his mother, not to one of His half-brothers. (James, the author of the book of James in the New Testament, was Jesus's brother). At this time, James was not a believer. James didn't become a believer until Jesus met him, one on one, in one of Jesus's postresurrection appearances.[13] I'd love to have been at that meeting.

John's Point of View

The primary point John is trying to make is to persuade us that Jesus Christ is the Messiah, the One sent by the Father as the sacrificial Lamb of God. The miracles of John's gospel do not point to Jesus's deity but to His Messiahship. Just before John the Baptist

---

[9] Matt. 17:1–9
[10] Luke 8:41
[11] Luke 9:28
[12] John 13:24–25
[13] 1 Corinthians 15:7

was beheaded, he sent his disciples to question Jesus one last time, *"Are you the One who was to come, or should we expect someone else?"*[14] Jesus's response wasn't, "Tell John, *yes* I'm the guy." It was, *"Go back and report to John what you hear and see: the blind receive sight, the lame walk, those who have leprosy are cured, the deaf hear, the dead are raised, and the good news is preached to the poor."*[15] Jesus referred to His miracles. Why? Because they were the proof that Jesus was indeed God's one and only Messiah.

Someone asked me the other day, "What's the difference in proving that Jesus is deity and Jesus is Messiah? Aren't they the same thing?" No, not exactly. *Deity* is a term that is synonymous with God. *Deity* means God who eternally exists. *Messiah* was the office of the One the Father would send as the Lamb of God to take away the sins of the world. There was only one Messiah, and He lived for thirty-three and a half years. He was God; Messiah was His office and mission.

This is the only account we have in the scriptures of the life of Jesus from His best and closest friend's point of view. That's what makes it so unique. John, instead of writing another synoptic, writes from a completely different frame of reference. John's is the most theological of all the gospels. He deals primarily with the nature and person of Christ and the meaning of placing our faith in Him. And there is much of the text of John that is not included in any of the other three gospels.

By the time John writes, all the other gospels have been written and widely circulated among the churches. All of Paul's books had been written as well as the books of Peter. These had been widely circulated. John is among the last of the New Testament books to be written. John most likely wrote from Ephesus around 90 AD after the destruction of Jerusalem in 70 AD.

---

[14]   Matthew 11:2–6
[15]   Matthew 11:5

His book contains no parables. He records only seven miracles, five of which are not found in the Synoptic, all pointing to the true identity of Jesus. They are the following:

1. Changing water into wine (John 2:1–11)*[16]
2. Healing the royal official's son in Capernaum (John 4:46–54)*
3. Healing the paralytic at Bethesda (John 5:1–18)*
4. Feeding the five thousand (John 6:5–14)
5. Walking on water (John 6:16–24)
6. Healing the man born blind (John 9:1–7)*
7. Raising of Lazarus from the dead (John 11:1–45)*

There are also the seven "I am" statements that only occur in the book of John. These also point to who Jesus really is, from Jesus's own mouth. They are the following:

1. I am the bread of life (John 6:35)
2. I am the light of the world (John 8:12)
3. I am the door of the Sheep (John 10:7)
4. I am the Good Shepherd (John 10:11)
5. I am the resurrection and the life (John 11:25)
6. I am the way, the truth, and the life (John 14:6)
7. I am the true vine (John 15:1)

A Simple Division

There are as many ways to outline this book as there are scholars to do so, so I will take a very simple approach. We are going to break the book of John into four main sections. It is my desire to make each section a separate commentary.

---

[16] The miracles marked * are only found in the gospel of John

Part 1, "Behold! The Man," will cover the lengthy introductory section of John's gospel in chapters 1–4. Here John introduces Jesus as the Word of God expressed in human flesh. The incarnation is the focus of this section. Jesus is introduced not only to the world, but to the nation of Israel. This is where we run into the witness of the Baptizer who was a remarkable figure in his own right. He was the one chosen to pave the way for the Messiah and His message.

Part 2, "Faith or Frustration," covers chapters 5–12. In this section, many of the multitudes are coming to believe in Jesus, much to the frustration of the Jewish leadership. As more and more believe, the Pharisees' curiosity turns to frustration; frustration slowly turns to anger; and finally, their anger develops into outright hatred. Their hatred culminates in a plot to have Him killed. The reason for their murderous hatred is expressed at a solemn meeting of the Great Sanhedrin in 11:48, *"If we let Him go on like this, all men will believe in Him!"* They felt compelled to kill Jesus, or they would lose their positions of power, privilege, and perhaps lose the nation itself. We will discover a direct parallel between the popularity of Jesus by the multitudes and the hatred of Him by the Jewish leadership.

Part 3, "Words to Loved Ones," covers chapters 13–17. In this section, Jesus has finished interacting with both the multitudes and the Pharisees. This time is devoted to His twelve men as He prepares them for His impending death. These five chapters cover a period of only about five hours just prior to Jesus arrest on the Mount of Olives. This is a time of great stress and confusion for the disciples. It is here, at the Last Supper, in the dim light of that Upper Room, that Jesus seeks to calm their "troubled hearts."[17] It is here Satan and God sit side by side! His death is less than twenty-four hours away.

Part 4, "The Failure of Death," our fourth and final section, covers chapters 18–21. In these pages, we will take a close look at both the events surrounding and including the crucifixion and the resurrection of Jesus. We will be among the crowd as they chant,

---

[17] John 14:1

15

"Crucify Him! Crucify Him!" We will hear the dull thud of the mallet as the nails are driven into His hands and feet; we'll hold Mary as she can barely contain her grief, trembling and sobbing uncontrollably; and we'll walk into that cold, dark, empty tomb with Peter and John. We will see what they saw that convinced them, "He is risen!" And we'll sit in shock and fear as He comes right through the door of our secret hiding place.

John's Purpose

Before we get into the book, one last comment about the reason John wrote his eyewitness, personal account of his very best friend. John very clearly states that reason at the end of the book in John 20:30–31. He says, "Many other signs therefore Jesus also performed in the presence of the disciples, which are not written in this book; but *these have been written that you may believe that Jesus is the Christ, the Son of God; and that believing, you may have life in His name.*"

According to this verse, John clearly did not record all the signs Jesus did during His ministry. In fact, he actually records only seven with any specificity. *Signs* literally means "attesting miracles." They are supernatural events, meaning beyond natural cause or explanation, but their purpose is to attest or draw attention to something (namely, that Jesus *was* the true Messiah of God, sent from the Father!).

Among whom did Jesus do these signs? Among the disciples and His followers. He didn't do them in a closet. He did them out in the open—in public, for all to see.

Why does John say he wrote about the signs he reveals in his book? He gives us two reasons. First, *"that you may believe that Jesus is the Christ"* (Messiah). John is writing to convince you that Jesus was in fact God's promised, anointed One. That He is the "Son of God," the Man/God who was one in essence with the Father. John wants you to come to believe the testimony of the Baptizer that Jesus was the true Lamb of God, and that through His sacrifice on the cross, forgiveness of sins was made available.

The second reason for writing was "*that believing, you may have life in His name.*" Not just living (eating, breathing, and sleeping), but LIFE, real life. John tells us in John 10:10 that Jesus came to give us "*life more abundant,*" and that is one of the major themes of this book. John uses the term *life* more than all the other gospels combined. It is a major theme of his book.

Jesus offers every one of us eternal life. That is not just a "pie in the sky in the sweet by and by" offer. He offers us the ability to live our lives today the way God intended us to live them. Lives that are characterized by peace in the midst of chaos, purpose in the midst of confusion, and meaning in the midst of hopelessness. He calls it "eternal life," and it starts TODAY!

As you "dig in," I hope you can feel the grit of the sand between your toes, smell the foul odors of the infirm around the pool of Bethesda, hear the desperation in the voice of the man born blind, see Lazarus stumble and almost fall as he emerges from his tomb still tightly bound by the burial cloths, experience the not-so-triumphal entry as our Lord weeps over the city, and feel the tears run down your own cheeks as you hold Jesus's trembling mother at the foot of the cross, listen to the hollow, rhythmic thud of the mallet as the spikes are driven through the flesh of your Master. You need to put your feet in their sandals, hear exactly what they heard, see what they saw, and smell what they smelled. Their fears and frustrations are yours. The hope they saw in Jesus is the hope that can be yours. Let God speak not just to your mind, but to your heart! Let your soul hear His Word.

Preface

Several months ago, my youngest son, Lance, came to me and told me that he felt like he wanted to learn more about the Bible. He asked if I would be willing to meet with him on a regular basis and study the Bible. So after discussing it a bit, we came to the conclusion that we would meet once a week and work our way systematically through the Gospel of John in the New Testament.

Lance is a third grade teacher at a local elementary school. We decided to meet every Thursday afternoon at 4:00 PM at a local espresso stand that had indoor seating for about twelve people. That would give him enough time to pick up his daughter at day care before heading home after our study.

We also agreed on a systematic approach to our study of John. First, we would predetermine how much of the text we would take before each meeting. We would start at chapter 1, verse 1 and simply work our way through the entire gospel. There were seven questions that we had predetermined we would ask of every text, every time. Those seven questions were the following:

> What does this teach me about God?
> What does this teach me about Jesus?
> What does this teach me about the Holy Spirit?
> Are there any promises to claim?
> Are there any commands to obey?
> Are there any sins to confess?
> What applications to my life can I make?

After answering the above questions, we would conclude with a section called "Questions and Comments." In this last section, we would ask any questions and make any comments that came to our minds. The sky was the limit. No questions, comments, or observations were out of bounds.

The result of this approach proved very interesting. First of all, we both discovered it took a considerable amount of discipline and time to go through those seven questions. In fact, more time and discipline than either of us actually had, given all our other commitments. My son was not only an elementary school teacher, but was also in a master's degree program, in theology, at Whitworth University here in Spokane. The course was very demanding.

But we did discover an interesting phenomenon with this approach. Having to carefully answer all seven questions forced us to actually read the text seven times. I discovered that if you read any text of scripture seven times carefully, all of a sudden, your mind begins to see things you've never seen before in the text. That brought to life the "Questions and Comments" section.

As we began to meet weekly, the "Questions and Comments: section became the heart and soul of our discussions. We looked at each text through the eyes of Jesus as he saw the multitudes hungering for truth but completely malnourished because of it, we felt the multitudes bumping and jostling into one another as they crowded to hear Him teach or heal, we looked into the faces of the folks whose lives were miraculously changed forever by His touch, and we crawled into the minds of the scribes and Pharisees and watched the panic slowly grip them as they felt themselves losing grip of the nation and the people to this carpenter from Nazareth. There were times we just sat in amazement at how it must have happened. There were other times we laughed until our sides ached as we considered certain scenes. (Can you imagine the scene as Lazarus tried to "walk" out of the tomb completely bound head to foot in grave cloths, hopping along, stumbling over rocks, bumping into the sides of the cave, almost landing on his face? You had to be there.)

After I wrote my first book, *Pagans, Prostitutes, and other Problems: A Simple Man's Commentary on Joshua*, Lance suggested that we coauthor a book. It was immediately obvious to me why he made that suggestion. Ever since Lance was a very young boy, he had both an aptitude and interest in writing. Carol, my wife, has saved some of his early writings. He is really quite gifted at it, so the idea made complete sense. Thus we decided to write a commentary on the Gospel of John. We've agreed to call it *Meet Messiah: A Simple Man's Commentary on the Gospel of John*, for that is what this gospel is all about. John introduces to us the God/Man named Jesus.

Unfortunately, Lance's schedule hasn't allowed him the time to commit to the writing, so I am going it alone. We still meet weekly and pick apart the text. It's been a rich experience for both of us. In addition, I've had the privilege of teaching through the book of John, at the same time I was meeting with Lance, to our Sunday school class at Valley Bible Church here in Spokane Valley, Washington. The class is very interactive with a lot of questions and discussion. I have been blessed by these faithful believers who've let me challenge their traditional thinking and who have equally challenged my "untraditional" thinking. They will never know how much they have meant to me.

There are not enough words to express my gratitude to Carol, who had both encouraged me in this project and had spent countless hours correcting my spelling, editing my material, and helping me communicate in a way real human beings normally communicate. It has been a herculean job for her, and she has done it selflessly. Thanks, sweetheart! I couldn't have done it without you.

Join us in our journey. You will enjoy the ride.

CHAPTER 1

God Spoke
John 1:1-5

Does Helen Keller ring any bell to you? She was born on June 27, 1880, and died on June 1, 1968 at eighty-seven years of age. At nineteen months of age, Helen contracted a disease that left her both blind and deaf. Many think it was either scarlet fever or meningitis. Her struggle to communicate is legendary and inspired the 1962 Hollywood movie *Miracle Worker*. Helen graduated in 1904 with a BA cum laude from Radcliffe College as the first blind-deaf person to ever graduate. She went on to receive honorary doctoral degrees from Temple University, Harvard, Universities of Glasgow, Berlin, Delhi, and Johannesburg.[18]

The isolation a blind-deaf person must live in is incomprehensible to me. No sound, no sight, no nothing for twenty-four hours a day, seven days a week for the rest of your life. After much struggle and incredible frustration and built-up anger, the breakthrough came for Helen when she finally associated Annie Sullivan, putting her hand under running water with Annie spelling the word *water* in her hand. The lightbulbs came on in Helen's mind so brightly, she couldn't get Annie to spell her enough words to make associations. In

---

[18] http://www.aph.org/hall/inductees/keller/

time, Helen Keller learned to speak. Helen became a prolific author, writing twelve books and numerous articles. Among the best was her own self-biography, *The Story of My Life*. *Words* changed Helen Keller's life.

It Can Be Said in a Word

The very first words of John's gospel are *"In the beginning."* So that is where we will start, at the beginning. Our intention is to work our way systematically through the Gospel of John, beginning to end. Hopefully, we will keep it simple and to the point.

In this four-part series *Meet Messiah*, we are calling Part 1 "Behold! The Man" This section will cover the first four chapters of the Gospel of John. These four chapters are a grand introduction of Jesus not just to the nation of Israel, but to the entire human race. Jesus is introduced to the human family in the first thirteen verses of chapter 1. Following that, the Baptizer, also named John, will introduce Jesus to the nation of Israel. So, let's get started by reading 1:1–5:

1. *In the beginning was the Word, and the Word was with God, and the Word was God.*
2. *He was in the beginning with God.*
3. *All things came into being by Him, and apart from Him nothing came into being that has come into being.*
4. *In Him was life, and the life was the light of men.*
5. *And the light shines in the darkness, and the darkness did not comprehend it*

Clearly, the focus of John's attention in this short paragraph is *"the Word."* Here, John tells us seven things about the Word:

1. The Word was in the beginning.
2. The Word was with God in the beginning.

3. The Word was God.
4. John refers to the Word in the first person singular (He, Him).
5. Everything that exists was created by the Word.
6. The origin of life existed within the Word.
7. The life of the Word was the light of men, which the darkness did not comprehend.

Wow! That's a mouthful and a lot to consider. Just about every one of the major themes in the gospel of John is mentioned here in the first five verses. Jesus, who is revealed as the Word in verse 14, is in fact God. Jesus is the source of all creation and rules over all, even the forces of nature. Jesus holds the secret of life for all of humanity. And He came to those who were His own, but because of the darkness, they misunderstood Him and failed to recognize who He was. These are just some of the themes introduced in these five verses.

The first question that probably comes to mind is, "Why does John refer to Jesus as 'the Word'?" It seems to me that the answer to that question is pretty intuitive.

If you were standing out on the front walkway of your house, like I was the other evening, and looked down and saw a million ants digging holes and "setting up shop" next to your house (like at mine), what would you do? If you lacked compassion for ants like I do, you'd get the ant spray out and give them a large dose of discouragement. But if for some weird reason you wanted to try to persuade them to go away, how would you do that? I'm sure there are many ways you could accomplish that, but one of the best ways would be to become an ant and go talk to them. You could let them know that if they didn't "move along," the spray was coming. In some sense, that is what God decided to do with us.

I suppose God could have communicated with humanity any number of ways. He could have spoken to us out of heaven like He did to His Son at His baptism. But that wasn't very effective, as many misunderstood Him. He could have written words on stone like

He did with Moses. But stones are cumbersome to pass around. He could have carved His words on the face of Half Dome in Yosemite National Park or on the Rock of Gibraltar in the Mediterranean. Or He could have used prophets to communicate to men as He did in the Old Testament times.

But God didn't want a "go-between" communicator. There was a much better way for God to communicate His Will to us. Words are the way we communicate with one another, either written or spoken, but words. Animals can communicate to some extent through grunts, growls, whines, and body expression. Only man, in every society throughout the world, in every culture and in every age, has developed the ability to communicate thought, will, and emotion very specifically with words.

Therefore, since God was desirous to communicate with us His character, love, and will, He chose to use the means by which He has created us to communicate—words! So before John identifies Jesus by name, he starts out by identifying how it is God has desired to communicate with us—through His Word, both spoken and written. And God wanted to speak to us in person, directly, face-to-face. That is the most effective way to communicate to someone you love.

There are three things in particular I'd like to draw your attention to about the Word in verse 1. The *first* thing John says about the Word is that the Word was "*In the beginning*." Notice that the statement "*in the beginning*" is repeated in verse 2 also, "*He was in the beginning with God*." Also, observe that John refers to the Word as *He* and *Him* using a first-person pronoun. The Word is not an inanimate object. The Word is not a doorknob. The Word is not an abstract concept or ideology. The Word is a *person*.

John is telling us that the Word existed *before* the beginning, before anything was created. This person, the Word, preexisted before both time and space, and He is eternal.

The *word*, or *logos*, simply means the written or audible expression of thought. But John is not talking in the abstract when he uses the first-person pronoun. He is telling us Jesus embodied the preexistent, eternal expression of the thought, mind, and heart of God.

By John using this familiar statement "*in the beginning*," there wasn't a first century Jew who wasn't familiar with the writings of Moses and that didn't understand John's intention. John was saying that the Word was the very same Person that Moses spoke of in Genesis 1 in describing the Creation account. The Creator in Genesis 1 is the same person as the Word in John 1.

The *second* thing John says about the Word is that the Word was "*with God*." This is where we run into a problem. "*With God*" means that the Word is distinct from the Father. They are two separate and distinct persons. Yet they are one in thought, meaning, and purpose. This is where our Mormon friends fall off the tracks.

Let me explain it like this. In Philippians 2:6, Paul says that Jesus existed "*in the form of God*." There are two Greek words for *form*. In Philippians 2:6–7, Paul uses the word *morphé* (mor-fa'). Let me define this Greek word *morphé* from *Strong's Dictionary.*

> *Morphé* denotes "the special or characteristic form or feature" of a person or thing; it is used with particular significance in the New Testament only of Christ in Philippians 2:6-7, in the phrases "being in the form of God," and "taking the form of a servant." An excellent definition of the word is that of Gifford: (Gifford writes) "*morphé*" is therefore properly the nature or essence, not in the abstract, but as actually subsisting in the individual, and retained as long as the individual himself exists...Thus in the passage before us *morphé Theou* is the Divine nature actually and inseparably subsisting in the Person of Christ...For the interpretation of "the form of God" it is sufficient to say that it includes the

whole nature and essence of Deity, and is inseparable from them, since they could have no actual
existence without it.

There is another word for *form* in the Greek. It is the word
schema. *Schema* is the outward expression of *form*, the expression that
you can see and touch. Schema can constantly change. *Morphé'* is
constant and unchangeable.

Here's a weak illustration, but I think makes the point. My *morphé* is who I really am. I have a body, but I am essentially soul and
spirit. The body I have today simply houses who I really am. And my
schema—or the expression of Paul Murray that you can see, hear,
and touch—has changed many times.

At one time my schema was expressed in the form of a baby.
Then it changed to a toddler. Then I became a young boy; next
a teenager, then a young man (quite good-looking, I might add).
Then I became a mature man. Now, I am an old, overweight (but
I am in shape; "round" is a shape), gray-haired man. But through
every form (schema), my essential nature (*morphé*) has never
changed.

John is saying that Jesus preexisted eternally with God and
His *morphé* was identical with the Father's *morphé*. They were two
persons but one in essence, nature, character, and will. They shared
identical *morphé*. John is telling us that God is one but expresses
Himself in three persons: the Father, the Son, and the Holy Spirit.
Jesus will tell the Jews in John 10:30, "*I and my Father are one.*" Jesus
couldn't be clearer. He is saying He and the Father are one and the
same, no difference. It is clear that the Jews understood exactly what
Jesus was saying because their response was "*The Jews took up stones
again to stone Him.*"[19]

---

[19] John 10:31

God or Man?

I want to go down a bit of a rabbit trail here. According to the biblical evidence, Jesus was fully God and fully Man all at the same time. The technical term for this dual nature is *hypostatic union*. I doubt if there are two Christians in two hundred that really believe that, although most would say they do. Let me ask you. Do you really believe that Jesus was all of God and all of man at the same time during His earthly life? Really?

If you believe that, let me ask you another question. Did Jesus have any advantage over you and me in living the Christian life? "Well, of course He did," many will argue. "He didn't have a sin nature. That had to be a great advantage. And besides, He was God. I have both a sin nature, and I'm certainly not God. So of course, Jesus had some advantages I don't have."

So here's the crucial question. Could Jesus have sinned? "Certainly not," is the typical response. "He was God. God cannot sin. The very definition of God is perfection. And that goes without question."

If you answered yes, that Jesus had an advantage that you don't have, yes, that Jesus having no sin nature gave Him a leg up in dealing with life that you don't have, and no, Jesus could never have sinned, then I submit that you *do not* believe that Jesus was fully God and fully Man in one schema, body.

I want you to consider carefully what Paul says about Jesus in Philippians 2:6–7:

6. *Who, although He existed in the form of God, did not regard equality with God a thing to be grasped,*
7. *but emptied Himself, taking the form of a bond-servant, and being made in the likeness of men*

What does Paul mean when he says Jesus *"emptied Himself?"* What exactly did Jesus empty Himself of? I would suggest that Jesus emptied Himself of at least five things.[20]

First, *He emptied Himself of His heavenly glory* when He entered the chaos, misery, and sewer of human existence. Jesus enjoyed the worship of angels in heaven. He was praised and adored. He was acknowledged and worshipped for who He really was.

In becoming a man, He gave up the worship of angels for the spittle of men. He chose to endure insults, beatings, humiliation, and suffering instead of honor and praise. In fact, in His High Priestly prayer in John 17:5 He prays, "Glorify Me together with you, Father, with the glory *which I had* with you before the world was." And on the Mount of Transfiguration, Jesus pulled back the flesh of his humanity and showed Peter, James, and John (this gospel writer) His true heavenly glory.

Second, *He emptied Himself of His independent authority to act as deity.* As Creator, Jesus ruled heaven and earth. He made everything and reigned as Lord and King over it all. But through the incarnation, He gave up that independent authority and rule. He tells us, in John 5:19, 30, and in several other passages in John's gospel, that He never acted on His own initiative. He only did what the Father showed Him to do. He submitted Himself to the authority of the Father even to the point of death on a cross.

Third, *He set aside His prerogatives of deity.* For example, He set aside His omnipresence, being everywhere at the same time. God is everywhere at the same moment. Jesus was not. Jesus was confined to time and space. Likewise, He set aside his prerogative of omniscience, His almighty power. He could only act as the Father empowered Him to act. Could He have acted in His own power? Of course, He was God. But He emptied Himself of that ability. He never once acted out of His deity. The miracles He did were not done because

---

[20] John McAuthor, <u>The Humiliation of Christ</u>, Philippians 2:5-8, November 6, 1988 50-16

He was God. They were done through His humanity as He trusted in the power of His Father to work miracles through Him.

Fourth, *He emptied Himself of His personal riches.* Paul tells us in 2 Corinthians 8:9 that *"though He was rich yet for our sakes He became poor, that through His poverty we might be made rich."* He had everything at His disposal in heaven. Yet He gave it all up that you might share in His riches. That is Paul's argument in Ephesians 1.

And finally, *He gave up His favored position with the Father.* He who knew no sin was made sin for us.[21] He cried out on the cross, *"My God, My God, why have you forsaken Me?"*[22] He who owned everything came to live among us as a servant. The Lord of glory had to borrow everything. He borrowed a place to be born, a place to lay His head daily, a boat to cross the sea, an animal for the triumphant entry, a room to celebrate Passover, and a tomb to be buried in. The only person who had the right to everything wound up with nothing so that we might gain everything! Praise God. He was fully God and fully Man in one person.

So, could Jesus have sinned? I may lose most of you here, but I certainly think He could have. He never did. But the reason He didn't wasn't because He was God. The reason He didn't was because He chose to do only what the Father showed Him to do. Jesus didn't sin because *He chose* not to sin. Have you ever been *forced* to sin? Have you ever been in a position where the only option you had was to sin? I think not. Even in the worst-case scenario, you sin because the consequences of not sinning is either perceived as too difficult or not as pleasurable as sinning. You sin because *you choose* to sin.

If Jesus had no possibility of ever sinning, then what were the temptations by the devil in the wilderness all about? Certainly, the devil would have known that if there was no possibility of Jesus sinning, why take Him into the wilderness? In fact, what's the point of any temptation if sinning is never a possibility. I'd love to be in that position.

---

[21] 2 Corinthians 5:21
[22] Mark 15:34

But I'm not. And I'm not because I'm a man. So was Jesus. Fully a man. How can I be in awe of Jesus for living a sinless life if He could have never sinned? I certainly can't follow His example because I can sin. I don't think the fact that Jesus could have sinned harms in any way the fact that He was also fully God. In fact, it enhances both aspects of His unique nature that He chose not to sin. That gives me hope. Maybe I too can choose not to sin the next time.

There is a *third* thing John says about the Word. John says, *"The Word was God."* John just simply lays it on the table. John doesn't say the Word "was a God" as the Mormons purport. That article *a* is nowhere in any of the original texts. The Mormons are just simply wrong in their version of the New Testament. This statement is the heart of Christianity. John is saying that the Word and God are one and the same in essence, purpose, and nature. As we stated above in John 10:30, Jesus makes this very claim Himself.

Jesus's Name

Jesus didn't get His name until His birth. Not even Joseph and Mary named their baby "Jesus." God decided to call His Son Jesus and gave instructions to the angel Gabriel to tell Mary that He was to be named Jesus.[23] *Jesus* means "Yahweh saves," which is the very reason God took on human flesh and became a man. But not only that, Gabriel went on to tell Mary that the Holy Offspring shall be called the Son of God.

Son of God is an amazing title that has been badly misunderstood in Western cultures. When you think of your son, you think of someone who may be like you in many respects, but a completely different personality. In the Jewish culture, they thought of the son as an identical replication or copy of the father in every respect. Therefore for a Jew, the Son of God did *not* mean someone like God.

---

[23] Luke 1:31

It meant someone identical to God in every respect; a coequal without exception, yet another.

There was no difference in essence or nature, only different in expression. We'll see this clearly illustrated as we go forward through the text. On a couple of occasions when the Jews picked up stones to stone Jesus, it was always because Jesus was saying that He was God. And they were clearly understanding Him to say that He was God. Not a god or a different god or a manifestation of God but actually God Himself. If the Jews thought that Jesus was claiming to be some other god than the one true God, they would never have sought to stone Him. Blasphemy was claiming to be *the* God, not some other god.

That is exactly what Gabriel was telling Mary. He was saying that her baby would be equal in every aspect with God. The reason Mary pondered these things in her heart was because she intellectually understood what Gabriel was saying, but she couldn't believe how it could be true. We'll get into this more later.

Darkness versus Light

In verses 4–5, John summarizes the whole purpose of the incarnation and the reason for it. Here, the whole drama of the gospel is also introduced. These two concepts, light and darkness, are a reflection of the good and evil that have pervaded the human race from the very beginning of time. Look how John states it in verses 4 and 5:

4. *In Him was life, and the life was the light of men.*
5. *And the light shines in the darkness, and the darkness did not comprehend it*

John tells us that Jesus was the very source of life itself. Life as God designed it to be lived. Life that was full of hope, purpose, potential, and all the possibilities of living above the fray of existence.

When John says, "*In Him was life,*" he means that without the life that He brings, men will by nature live in a state of darkness.

Jesus was not just the author of physical life. What John is referring to is something much deeper. He is not referring to "being alive." He is not referring to just mere existence. John is talking about *living* with a capital *L*. Jesus Himself says in John 10:10 that He came that we "*might have life and have it more abundantly.*" That's what Jesus came to offer every one of us, "life *more abundant.*" Is that what you are experiencing today? You can! It's freely available.

What is the life that Jesus says is "*abundant life?*" The term that we find repeated over and over again in John's gospel that describes this life is the term *eternal life.* When Jesus or John use the term *eternal life*, they are not simply talking about living a long time. In just about every instance of the use of that term, the context has to do with quality of life, not length of life.

In a nutshell (and this will be clarified much more in John 5:19 and following), Jesus came to deliver us from darkness. Darkness is a metaphor for all the ramifications of life without Christ that every one of us struggles with on a daily basis. He came to free us from the guilt of our mistakes, the frustration of our failures, the confusion of our thinking, and shame of our sin. He came to empower us through the greatest gift ever offered to men, the Holy Spirit. Through the indwelling power of the Holy Spirit, God can empower us to live above the crushing pressures of life. He will empower us to walk by the Spirit and not by the flesh. And the "frosting on the cake" is the guarantee of life with Him for all eternity beyond the grave. There is life after death. The whole direction of your life on this earth sets in motion the direction of where you will spend your eternal existence.

That is eternal life. That is the life that was in Him. That is the life He came to offer all men. And that is the life that every one of us can begin to enjoy immediately. Eternal life, quality of life, begins the moment we receive Him as our Lord and Savior. And it is ours throughout this life and on into the next. That was the life (and the gift) that was in Him.

Jesus's life on earth was truly amazing. One astute writer expressed it in a short essay called,

"One Solitary Life"[24]

Here is a man who was born in an obscure village, the child of a peasant woman. He grew up in another village. He worked in a carpenter shop until He was thirty. Then for three years He was an itinerant preacher.

He never owned a home. He never wrote a book. He never held an office. He never had a family. He never went to college. He never put His foot inside a big city. He never traveled two hundred miles from the place He was born. He never did one of the things that usually accompany greatness. He had no credentials but Himself...

While still a young man, the tide of popular opinion turned against him. His friends ran away. One of them denied Him. He was turned over to His enemies. He went through the mockery of a trial. He was nailed upon a cross between two thieves. While He was dying His executioners gambled for the only piece of property He had on earth—His coat. When He was dead, He was laid in a borrowed grave through the pity of a friend.

Nineteen long centuries have come and gone, and today He is a centerpiece of the human race and leader of the column of progress.

I am far within the mark when I say that all the armies that ever marched, all the navies that

---

[24] This essay was adapted from a sermon by Dr. James Allan Francis in *The Real Jesus and Other Sermons* © 1926 by the Judson Press of Philadelphia (pp 123–124 titled "Arise, Sir Knight!").

were ever built; all the parliaments that ever sat and all the kings that ever reigned, put together, have not affected the life of man upon this earth as powerfully as has that one solitary life.

The Light of Men

Before we conclude, John makes another significant claim about this life. He says, "The life [that Jesus possessed] was the light of men." John's meaning is very simple, yet profound. The simplicity is in all that Jesus said and did, He demonstrated to every one of us *how* God intended life to be lived. He answers the three most driving questions of humanity:

Who am I?
Why am I here?
Where am I going?

Jesus's life *enlightens* every man to these three realities. John states in verse 5 how Jesus's life dispels the darkness and makes things visible. Through the example of Jesus's life and the wisdom of His teaching, He illuminates things so we can see them as they really are. He clears up confusion and answers our questions. He reveals to us how God intended life to be lived. And He does this by answering the three questions above.

The truth that John is making in the statement *"The light shines in the darkness"* is that all men live in darkness. We think we are enlightened, educated, and sophisticated. But since the fall, men have always lived in darkness. Jesus came into a world of darkness. The Apostle Paul says *all have sinned* and fallen short of the glory of God.[25] *All* means *all.* Paul goes on to say none were righteous, not

---

[25] Romans 3:23

even one.[26] And that the wages of their sin, which is death,[27] has weighed heavily upon all of us.

Sin has created a dark, heavy pall over mankind. Jesus came to penetrate that darkness and bring light into a dark world. By revealing to men how God had intended all men to live life, He brings hope to the hopeless, help to the helpless, life to the lifeless, and grace to those who have given up. That's the Light that was in the Life of Jesus

Verse 5 also introduces a conflict that has gone on since the beginning of time. This conflict will be clearly revealed from chapter 5 onward in this gospel. And it is a conflict between light and darkness, between good and evil, between God and Satan, and between right and wrong.

The problem that the darkness has with the Light is that the darkness can't "comprehend" the Light or extinguish it or overpower it (depending on your translation). The meaning is, literally, "cannot get hold of it" or "cannot lay hold of it" or "cannot take control of it."

The typical human reaction to something we cannot comprehend or understand or figure out is generally to fear it or reject it. Because we don't understand, we put labels on those things we can't comprehend as foolish.

This is why the apostle Paul says in 1 Corinthians 2 that *"the natural man [unbeliever] does not accept the things of the Spirit of God, for they are foolishness to him, and he cannot understand them, because they are spiritually appraised."* John will tell us in chapter 3 *why* the darkness cannot comprehend the light.

Isn't it interesting that light drives darkness away? Darkness cannot drive light away. You can shine light into darkness, but you can't shine darkness into light. You can cover light, you can extinguish a flame, you can put a box over a lamp, you can turn a light switch off, but you can't turn darkness off. The only way to dispel darkness is to introduce light.

---

[26] Romans 3:10
[27] Romans 6:23

Here, we are just introduced to the conflict between light and darkness, and it is a conflict that will go on until the end of time. But at the end of the story, the Light will ultimately triumph.

Application

So what is John driving at in his opening five verses? God has spoken to men in his own language, through His Word. God has spoken so that men may know how to live life as life was intended to be lived. But before a man will ever understand _anything_, he must first come to realize and recognize that he is in darkness. Without that first step of honest recognition, no man will ever comprehend the Light. And they will be confined to live out their lives and their eternity in darkness.

If you have never admitted that you are in darkness, now is the time to start. Start by humbly coming before God and honestly confessing to Him that you have lived your life in darkness. Admit to Him that you don't have all the answers to all of your struggles. In fact, confess that you don't really have any of the answers to any of your struggles. Then ask Him to begin to shed the light of the truth of His life into your heart and mind. And begin to allow Him to wash you with the light of His gospel. Then read on!

CHAPTER 2

You're Not Welcome!

John 1:6-13

Remind me not to go to high school reunions anymore. (And I've only been to one!) About five years ago, I went to my fiftieth. I know, am I really that old? It was held in a Marriott Hotel in Newport Beach, California. We were the class of 1961 from Newport Harbor High. Go, Tars!

Carol and I were supposed to go together, but the day before we were to leave, Carol came down with pneumonia. As the reservations had already been made and paid for, we discussed it, and I wound up going down by myself. I was to meet up in the lobby of the Marriott with my best friend from high school, a kid I haven't seen in almost fifty years. He and his wife were coming from Chandler, Arizona.

I got to the Marriott about an hour before we were to meet and signed in. Thank goodness, our nametags had pictures of what we looked like as high school Seniors. I could recognize NO ONE! I was shocked by all the Botox, platinum hair, lifts, and whatever else has been designed to stretch and pull skin tight or cover wrinkles and make the hair of a seventy-year-old look like it should be on a teen-ager (or a Barbie doll)!

Now, I'm not trying to be critical here, nor am I trying to be the "pot calling the kettle black." This old body I hang around in has had a lot of tread wear. What used to be my chest is now my stomach. I'm grateful I still have my hair, but it's turned a strange color of "dirty gray." But what I have is all natural. Having said that, maybe I should try using some "improvements."

The real shocker, though, was when my friend came in. I was standing in the plush lobby admiring the glitter of the sun reflecting off the water of the Back Bay out the floor-to-ceiling windows. Behind me, I heard his voice, "Paul!" I recognized that voice immediately. It hadn't changed one bit. How refreshing, I thought, some things never change.

I turned to greet him, but he was nowhere in sight. Again, I heard my name, "Paul!" It was him, again. The sound was coming from right in front of me. But where was he? I looked in every direction. Then a third time, "Paul." I stared intently at the person I thought said my name. As his wife walked up to him, I recognized her immediately. She hadn't changed a bit, at least not much. Then I looked back. It *was* Bob. As I looked at him, he had obviously aged (as all of us had), but I don't think I could have picked him out of a crowd of three! Almost immediately, all the familiar recognitions began to come back. The three of us greeted and hugged. We were inseparable for the weekend. As we spent time together, everything came back and fell into place. It was the same old Bob. Gracious to a fault, kind, loving, crazy, and so much fun to be with. The outside may have changed over time, but the inside was perfectly preserved, if not fine-tuned into a more compassionate human being. What a great reunion that was just seeing the two of them again.

As we come to verse 6 of chapter 1, we arrive at a scene that briefly describes a similar kind of awkwardness as the God who created everything comes to dwell among His own creation. He was as unrecognizable to His own as my old friend was to me at my fiftieth reunion.

The Witness

The Apostle John begins by introducing us to another John:

6. *There came a man, sent from God, whose name was John*
7. *He came for a witness, that he might bear witness of the light, that all might believe through him*
8. *He was not the light, but came that he might bear witness of the light.*

Here we are introduced to the one who is known as John the Baptist. We will see a lot of him in the next few chapters. He is quite an amazing character. This introduction is very simple and very straightforward.

The first thing we learn about John was that he was *"sent from God."* The record of John the Baptist's unique birth is extensively recorded in Luke 1. The Old Testament prophets had predicted that a prophet would arise in Israel prior to the coming of the Messiah.[28] The angel of the Lord told Zacharias before John's birth that John would be the forerunner to the Messiah and would have a ministry in the same spirit as Elijah.[29] He would be one who would call the nation of Israel to repent for their sins. Jesus Himself recognized John as the fulfillment of that angelic prediction.[30] So there is no question that God had uniquely set John apart for a special ministry as the one who would prepare the way for the coming of the Messiah.[31]

But let me pause for a moment unless we miss a very important and fundamental point. How about you? Yes, *you*! Are you special? Are you sent from God? Do you have a unique purpose and place in life as John had?

---

[28] Deuteronomy 18:15, 18
[29] Luke 1:17
[30] Matthew 11:14
[31] John 1:23

I think most of us think of ourselves as pretty ordinary, mundane, vanilla-type Christians. Nothing special here. Just an old saint swinging the bat, day in and day out, trying to hit the ball. But wait a minute. Let me challenge that attitude. At the end of this book, our Savior issues a challenge to the apostles that, by association, is transferred to every one of us as believers. In one of His very last postresurrection appearances, Jesus says, *"As the Father has sent Me, I also send you."*

This is the Great Commission passage in the book of John. It is found in all four gospels. That fact alone makes it an extremely important passage. *You* are a "sent one" by God in every bit the same sense that John the Baptist was sent by God. You have been commissioned by your Lord as His personal ambassador.[32] That is an extremely high calling. You are His chosen instrument to touch those in your sphere of influence for Him. That's not a calling you share; that's a calling you *own!*

The name *John* means "gift of God." Your name may not mean "gift of God," but I hope you realize that God has gifted you as His representative to be in every sense His gift to those you come in contact with and are touched with the grace He has given you.

The Baptizer's mission was, in a real sense, the same mission we all have as ambassadors of Christ. *"He came for a witness, that he might bear witness of the light, that all might believe through him."* That's a pretty lofty goal, that *all might believe* through him. It was John's purpose to be a witness of the light. The truth is, that is *your* purpose and mine as well.

Real Success

I would like to make a comment about the "success" of John's ministry. Did *all believe* through John that Jesus was the true light? Of course not. In fact, many rejected John's witness including the

---

[32] 2 Corinthians 5:20

most religious elite of the day. The ultimate result of John's witness to the light was that he got his head cut off, literally! Now, there's a real measure of success!

You might ask if John really, successfully fulfilled his mission. From a human perspective, men measure success or failure by *accomplishment*. Success is determined by whether we win or lose, whether we achieve a preset goal, whether we get the most votes.

But God doesn't measure success from man's point of view. God measures success or failure by *obedience or faithfulness*. Results are not our concern. Results are God's prerogative. If we trust and obey, then the will of God is accomplished regardless of what that looks like to us. Do you see the difference? Men measure success or failure by what they achieve; God measures success or failure by obedience.

My experience witnessing with Campus Crusade was very humbling. As a college student, every Monday, Wednesday, and Friday, we would go out on campus at San Jose State College to share the *Four Spiritual Laws* with students. The *Four Spiritual Laws* was an effective little booklet we used to share the gospel message in a simple and understandable way. Most of the time, I felt like a failure. The majority of students I shared with weren't really interested. And I've never handled rejection well, so I would wind up feeling pretty discouraged.

Occasionally, there would be someone that was genuinely interested in wanting to be a Christian. There was one particular instance when a group of us involved with Campus Crusade had gone to Santa Cruz, California, for spring break. Our purpose was to share our faith with students who had come to the beach for their spring break vacation.

I had engaged one young man, who seemed really interested in the *Four Spiritual Laws*. The "transition" statement at the end of the presentation was, "Is there any reason why you wouldn't want to ask Christ into your life right now?"

The young man I was speaking with, sitting on a towel at the beach alone, looked up at me and said, "This is really amazing!"

43

"What is?" I replied. He responded, "I'm the associate pastor of a Presbyterian church. I've graduated from seminary. I thought I was pretty knowledgeable about the Bible. But no one has ever told me that I could have a *personal relationship* with Jesus Christ. I would like to pray and ask Him into my life."

So, we prayed together. After chatting for a while longer, I left him. I've never seen or heard from him again. Neither of us had a pen or pencil to get the other's number. The Lord only knows where he is today. I've always considered that a really special divine encounter.

Then it finally dawned on me. Success wasn't in the number of people that responded positively to my attempts to share my faith. Success was in the very fact that I was attempting to share my faith. The truth of Paul's statement in 2 Corinthians 2:14 hit me in a whole new, significant way: "*But thanks be to God, who <u>always</u> leads us in His triumph in Christ, and manifests through us the sweet aroma of the knowledge of Him in every place.*" Before we would go out on any given day to share our faith with complete strangers, we would spend time in prayer, asking the Father to lead us to those with whom He wanted us to speak.

Before this encounter with the Presbyterian pastor, I don't think I ever believed that God was really doing that. How could the majority of folks I sought to share with not be interested if God was leading me to share with those He wanted me to speak to? But then I realized, being open or closed to what I was sharing had nothing to do with it. The issue wasn't the results. The issue was the obedience, the very fact that I was willing to share my faith. I certainly have no idea where any of those conversations ultimately went. Only God knows. And only God needs to know. Now I'm certainly no evangelist, but that is not the point at all. It is God who leads us *in His triumph* every time, without exception, when we are willing to walk by faith and trust Him. What that means is that not one of those experiences, regardless of the rejection, was a failure. It was all a triumph in Christ.

I often wonder how John felt. He had great crowds coming to him to be baptized, multitudes, and that must have been an encouragement. But John's ministry was very controversial. The smart and sophisticated people were very skeptical. Almost the entire Jewish intellectual community, the scholarly Jewish religious leadership, rejected John after interviewing him. I say, "OUCH!" That must have hurt.

The author, John, makes very clear in verse 8 that John the Baptist was not the true light, but he bore witness of the light. In verses 9–13, John clarifies and defines the purpose of the light:

9. *There was the true light which, coming into the world, enlightens every man.*
10. *He was in the world, and the world was made through Him, and the world did not know Him.*
11. *He came to His own, and those who were His own did not receive Him.*
12. *But as many as received Him, to them He gave the right to become children of God, even to those who believe in His name,*
13. *who were born not of blood, nor the will of the flesh, nor of the will of man, but of God.*

Which Light?

What do you think the implication of John's statement in verse 9 is when he says, "There was the true light?" What does the term *true light* imply? It is an acknowledgment that there are false lights or imitation lights. There are those that masquerade as light but are liars and deceivers. You don't have to look far across the landscape of religion to see all those claiming to be the proprietors of the light and truth. The list of such "truth tellers" is almost endless: from the Mormons to the Jehovah's Witnesses, Seventh-Day Adventist, Christian Scientist, Scientologists, Jews, Hindus, Buddhism, and even to the many denominations of evangelical Christendom. All claim to have the real truth, the light. Sunday-night television is filled with preachers of every color and stripe, most asking for your money or promising you holy water that will fix all your ills. No wonder Pilate asked Jesus that eternal question, "What is truth?"

Here, in chapter 1, John tells us exactly what the "true light" really is. It is not an ideology, it's not a doctrine, it's not a statement of faith. It's not even a religious order, sect, or denomination. The true light is none other than a Person. Specifically, the true light is the person of Jesus Christ, who was the Word that became flesh to dwell among us.

John says that when Jesus came into the world, He "enlightens every man." I hope you see that the text doesn't say that He "convinces every man." It just says He "enlightens every man."[33] That means that Jesus coming into the world has presented every man with a very clear choice.

What Jesus has done is to reveal to humanity who God is and what God desires of each one of us. Jesus reveals not only the nature and character of God but also the mind, will, and plan of God. Jesus came to seek and to save that which was lost[34]—you and me! He offers us a way of escape from our old sinful nature. He offers to restore the relationship with God that our own personal sin has destroyed. He offers to pay the "sin" debt we've incurred in full so that we might have a personal relationship with God through Him. He offers to give us His Spirit to live within us to lead us and guide us into all truth.

The Apostle Paul argues in Romans that one of the ways God has been revealing Himself to us from the beginning of time is through the conscience of man. Every man is born with a conscience. It's your conscience that makes you feel good or bad about your behavior. It's your conscience that makes you feel "funny or awkward" about doing something. It's your conscience that points a guilty finger at you and makes you feel ashamed when you know you've blown it.

The scriptures are clear in an abundance of passages that we all start out with a clear, clean conscience. Our conscience provides that

---

[33] John 1:9
[34] Luke 19:10

initial internal acknowledgement of right and wrong. It is one of the vehicles the Holy Spirit uses to lead us to the Savior. So keep it clean and clear.

However, through a process of choices, we can destroy our conscience. The Bible says in 1 Timothy 4:2 that you can sear your conscience. Paul says in 1 Corinthians 8:7 that your conscience can become weak and defiled. You can also wound your conscience[35] and it can become evil.[36]

One of the most interesting facts about man is that he is the only animal on the planet that worships! Every tribe in every nation around the entire globe has practiced some form of worship from the very beginning of time. Man, from birth, internally acknowledges a supreme being. Man has a God consciousness. No other animal prays. All men instinctively know there is a "higher power," whether they try to deny it or not. We'll hear a little later from John that men love darkness rather than light.[37] That explains why our conscience gets twisted and confused, and that explains why our worship becomes degraded and ugly.

As Jesus reveals the truth (turns on the light) of who God really is, man is left with a choice. Will I believe Jesus, or will I reject what He says? It is based on that choice that every human who has ever existed will stand before the judgment seat of God to determine his or her eternal destiny. It's a good idea not to get that one wrong!

John tells us in verse 10 that He was in *"the world..."* and *"the world did not know Him."* How humbling it must have been for the very Creator to come among His own creation and not be recognized by them. Verse 10 is a general reference to all of creation, including men everywhere. In verse 11, John says he came to *"His own,"* meaning His own people, the Jewish people. These were the descendants of Abraham. These were the ones Jesus had made promises to through their forefathers, beginning with Abraham. Jesus had prom-

---

[35] 1 Corinthians 8:12
[36] Hebrews 10:22
[37] John 3:19

ised that through Abraham's seed He would bless the entire world. And here He is, the seed of Abraham, the One promised to bless the world. Here is their deliverer, and they didn't recognize Him, nor did they receive him.

In verse 12, John paints with a broad brush the purpose of the Messiah he is introducing. *"His own"* in verse 11 is a reference to the children of Israel, the chosen people of God. They considered themselves, and only themselves, as the "children of God." It was to those the promises of God had been made. Yet in verse 12, John tells us *"As many as receive Him, to them He gave the right to become the children of God, even those who believe on His name."*

Receive Him?

Can that be true? Is God giving anyone, even Gentiles, Samaritans, and barbarians, the right to become the children of God if they receive Jesus? That would be an absurd thought to any Jew! Because it could also mean that if a Jew *didn't* receive Him, then that Jew would not be a child of God, regardless of heritage or promise. I hope you can see the controversy this would create in the minds of the Jews.

The last phrase of verse 12 explains what *"receive Him"* means. It means to *"believe in His name."* Believing in someone's name does not mean believing in bits and pieces of what they say, accepting some things, and rejecting others. It means embracing them lock, stock, and barrel. It means all or none at all. So many people today tell me they believe in this or that about Jesus. But they just can't accept some of this other stuff. That's not John's concept of believing in His name. For John, Jesus comes as a *whole*. If you don't take it all, you can't have any of it. Sorry!

In verse 13, John defines the universality of who those are who believe in His name. He begins by describing what they are not. First, he says, a child of God is *not* someone *"born of blood, nor the will of the flesh, nor of the will of man."*

That is a broad and sweeping statement. By *"born of blood,"* John is saying that your "pedigree" does not get you into heaven or make you a child of God. Being a Jew or an American or a Baptist or a Catholic gets no one into heaven or into God's graces. By *"will of the flesh,"* John is saying there is nothing you can do through human effort, through the works of the flesh, that will earn you a place in God's kingdom. All the philanthropy, all the volunteerism, all the good works, all the church going, all the charitable deeds that you will ever do goes nowhere is getting you any closer to God. By *"the will of man,"* John is simply summarizing that *no* human effort will ever gain you a position as a child of God. Man *cannot* get there in and of himself or by any of his own efforts.

Just because you were born a Jew gives you no special privilege in becoming a child of God. Just because you were born the child of a pastor does not make you a child of God. Just because you were born an American, raised in a Christian family, went to church all your life *does not* make you a Christian. In fact, nothing about heritage, bloodline, or any human association has anything to do with you being a child of God. Again, you cannot become a child of God through human effort of any kind, regardless of how loving, kind, and generous you are. I don't know how John could have driven this point home more strongly.

Then he very simply states what *is* necessary to become a real child of God. He says you *must* be *"born of God."* It is that simple; end of story. Of course, you might ask, "How can I be born of God?" I'm glad you asked. Nicodemus is going to ask that same question of Jesus in chapter 3 of John's gospel.

Again, quite simply as John stated in verse 12, you must "receive Him." As described above, to receive Him means that you embrace by faith not only who He is but all that He claims and promises. It is a matter of placing your complete trust and faith in Jesus Christ as your Lord and your Savior. That and that alone is the only requirement for becoming a child of God. To add anything to that (including baptism or catechism or not smoking or drinking) is to adulterate and make dirty the salvation Jesus offers. To take anything away from it is to miss it completely. As we've stated, it is all or nothing at all.

Paul states it this way: *"For by grace you have been saved through faith; and that not of yourselves, it is the gift of God; not as a result of works, so that no one may boast."*[38]

Application

John bore witness to the true Light, the One who shines the light of truth into our dark and weary lives. A light that reveals who we are without Him and what we can be if we will only embrace Him fully. That light of truth seen in Jesus Christ gives every one of us a choice. It is a choice to live in the light of His glorious grace or to continue to dwell in the darkness of our own creation. We will all make that choice, either by a deliberate act of our will or by simply doing nothing and trying to ignore it. That too is a choice. Choose wisely.

---

[38] Ephesians 2:8–9

CHAPTER 3

Hi! My Name Is Jesus
John 1:14-18

Do you have a best friend? I mean, someone you are really close to, who you are completely comfortable being around. I'm talking about someone that lifts your spirit, challenges your thinking, and someone with whom you can be yourself, warts and all?

If there is, I'd like you to get a very clear mental picture of him or her in your mind. What are they like? How do they dress? What is their demeanor around you? How do they express their attitudes and character? What do they look like? How do they interact with others? Can you get a clear picture of that person in your mind?

Now, I'd like you to climb into an imaginary scene with me. Imagine that you are one of Jesus's twelve disciples and that Jesus of Nazareth was your very best friend. You had just spent the last three and one-half years with Him as you wandered the countryside of Judea, Samaria, and Galilee together. You have spent almost every waking hour with Him. Are you still with me? OK, now describe Him as clearly and in as much detail as you can.

If I had been one of the twelve, here is how I would describe Him:

He was about five feet ten inches tall, had a dark complexion, and was built about normal for His size. He weighed in around 163 pounds and had dark-brown eyes. His dress was not fancy, mostly typical for the area. In a crowd of fifty men, you would be hard-pressed to pick Him out among them. There were no unusual characteristics about Him.

He was both fun and scary to be with. Not scary like being afraid, but scary like being uncomfortable at times. He certainly wasn't a bore, and He never looked for a fight, although He was not afraid of confrontation. He was a little too unpredictable for my taste. You never knew what He would do next.

He seemed to be tender to the unfortunate people most of us ignore or never think of much. He was patient with honest inquirers but seemed elusive and indirect with those He thought weren't really listening to Him. His honesty with folks often made me uncomfortable. Political correctness didn't seem to be His "long suit." He was not afraid to expose very respectable clergymen for their hypocrisy. He openly called King Herod a fox, not very flattering and a pretty dangerous thing to do. He easily went to parties with many who were considered "disreputable people." The established taboos of mingling with "publicans and sinners" didn't seem to bother Him. Working on the Sabbath was no big deal to Him, and oh, how that angered the Pharisees. I guess you could say He wasn't too concerned about what people thought of Him. But if He thought you were insulting His Father, watch out!

He would go places I wasn't comfortable going. His assault on the temple, both times, was, from my point of view, pretty much out of line. For my money, it was too impetuous. I'm sure there could have been a better way to handle that situation. Yet there was a lot of corruption and extortion going on in the temple. I'm sure a proper report to the appropriate authorities would have been a better approach than the havoc He caused. I thought for sure the temple guards would arrest us all.

It was shocking when He cured diseases and folks that were crippled, blind, or lame. He did it so effortlessly. There was hardly any fanfare, nor did He make a big deal out of it. There was no shouting to the Father, "Heal!" No long prayers or pleading with God. No "laying on of hands" for the most part. He just quietly spoke a word, and sometimes didn't even do that. He did it like I would offer a candy sucker to a child. "Here. Take it. Have a nice day."

The crowds were stimulating and sometimes frightening. They all seemed to be eager to be near Him. I hated that claustrophobic feeling. The scribes and the Pharisees were always up front, watching every move. But I could never figure out their motives. Most of the time it felt like they were there just to see what He would do next. And every time He healed someone, the Jewish leadership would frantically begin mumbling amongst themselves. They never seem happy for the person Jesus healed. That always struck me as odd.

I honestly wonder how many true, trusted friends He had. He often seemed almost aloof from people, not disengaged but not really trusting either. Common people seemed to love Him. Smart people seemed to hate Him. I could never understand that conundrum.

The thing that made me the most uncomfortable around Him was that he treated people all the same, regardless of whether they were rich or poor. I couldn't understand how He could do that. People need to earn respect, don't they? It was clear by His actions and behavior that He was really a good guy at heart. When I compare Him with myself, it makes me cringe. But I have never gotten the feeling that He looked down on me.

Your Tent

Look what John says about Jesus in verse 14:

14. *And the Word became flesh, and dwelt among us, and we beheld His glory, glory as of the only begotten from the Father, full of grace and truth.*

Clearly, this is the verse where John is describing the incarnation of Jesus. *"The Word became flesh, and dwelt among us."* The *incar-*

nation is a term that refers to God taking on human form, flesh. The phrase *dwelt among us* literally translates "tabernacled among us or tented among us." What John is telling us is that when Jesus (who eternally preexisted with God in heaven) became a man, He took on flesh or a "tent." Jesus's physical form was the "tent" that contained the real Jesus. It was the tent that contained the soul and spirit of Jesus. Tabernacles (like the one during the forty years of wandering of the Jew in the Old Testament) and tents are temporary structures, just like our bodies are temporary structures.

Now, don't let me lose you here. John is only stating the obvious for every person that ever existed. Your body is *your* tent. The real you isn't your physical body. That "thing" that looks out of your eyeballs, that expresses your thoughts and emotions, is the real you. We call it our soul or spirit. Your soul is not physical, nor is your spirit. But without your body, your soul and spirit have no way of expressing themselves, right? When someone dies, his or her soul and spirit doesn't die. That nonphysical part of us lives on forever. But without a body, you have no ability to express yourself.

That's exactly why the Apostle Paul didn't want to be without some kind of tent, either earthly or heavenly, because without it he wouldn't be able to express himself. Paul didn't want to be "unclothed."[39] Look how Paul describes this concept in 2 Corinthians 5:1–4. Paul uses the term *tent* to describe his body, either earthly or heavenly. He tells us, "*For we know that if the earthly tent which is our house is torn down* [he is referring to his physical body there]*, we have a building from God* [he's referring to his post-resurrection glorified body here]. *For indeed while we are in this tent, we groan.*" We all have our "tents." Some of your tents look pretty nice. My tent is sadly much larger than it should be. The point is, the "tent" is not the real you! The tent is nothing more than the clothing that houses your soul and spirit as we've said. Your tent allows your soul and spirit to express itself.

---

[39] 2 Cor. 5:4

In describing the tent that Jesus took on, there was one primary thing that struck John's attention. He saw the glory of Jesus's character. The only way John could describe the soul and spirit of Jesus was that it was *"glory as of the only begotten from the Father, full of grace and truth."* The two terms that summarized for John the glory of the character of Jesus was that He was full of *grace* and *truth*. Jesus's entire life was an expression and manifestation of grace and truth as expressed by the Father.

Grace and Truth

Most Christians would agree that a good, simple definition of *grace* is expressed in the acrostic: GRACE = God's resources at Christ's expense. It is unmerited favor, the love of God poured out to sinful men who rightly deserve nothing but the condemnation and judgment of God. Jesus was *full* of grace. It was the attitude with which He approached all men.

We will see, through our study of this gospel, Jesus's unlimited willingness to love the unlovely, touch the untouchable, dine with the despised. He became known as the friend of sinners. And to those who would express true repentance and trust in Him as their Messiah, He offered complete, unmerited, total forgiveness with *no* strings attached. Thank God, because I was one of those!

He was also full of truth. *Truth* is defined as the way God sees things. Truth is discovered not through the scientific process, but through divine revelation. Truth is the manifestation of reality as God has defined and described it. It's the stripping away of all illusions and facades. Truth is quite simply what God says about reality. You will notice as we go through this study how many times Jesus "deliberately" worked on the Sabbath in what the Jews believed was a direct violation of the Mosaic law. We will discover that the reason Jesus did this was directly tied to the truth that He would not compromise. His uncompromising commitment to the truth was the main reason He was crucified.

If you want to establish a life goal, something that you would like to be known for, I suggest to set your sights on this goal: seek to be the kind of person where everything that comes out of your mouth, and every action you do is a balance of "grace and truth!" Many are good with demanding the truth, but they are almost completely devoid of grace. They are harsh and rigid in their commitment to truth and express little love or compassion. Others exude grace, compassion, and empathy in abundance; but they seem to avoid the truth completely, not wanting to be offensive. "Speak the truth in love" is just a cliché for most. It needs to be a way of life.

John expands on this idea of "grace and truth" in verses 15–17. John turns to John the Baptist's testimony and makes this point in verse 15:

15. *John bore witness of Him, and cried out, saying, "This was He of whom I said, 'He who comes after me has a higher rank than I, for He existed before me.'"*

To the Jews, this statement made no sense at all. John the Baptist was saying that Jesus was of higher rank than he, meaning that Jesus was John the Baptist's elder, both in age and stature. John was saying that Jesus existed before him. We know from the parallel accounts of the gospels that John the Baptist was actually six months *older* than Jesus.[40] The Jews were clearly aware of this. The only way Jesus could have preexisted the Baptizer was if He truly was the Eternal One, who existed before the world was created. To the Jews, it was a conundrum. To John, it was a statement of the deity of Jesus.

John goes on to tell us what that meant to him in 16–17:

16. *For of His fullness we have all received, and grace upon grace.*
17. *For the Law was given through Moses; grace and truth were realized through Jesus Christ.*

---

[40] Luke 1:36

The term John the Baptist uses, "*grace upon grace*," means "grace piled upon grace," "abundant grace," "multiplied grace," "grace added to grace." John is saying that grace without measure has been poured out in all of our lives, believer and nonbeliever alike.[41] The evidence comes in two forms. First of all, we have all sinned and fallen short of the glory of God, as we've seen earlier. And the wages of that sin is the eternal judgment of God. Well, if you are still drawing breath and are not a Christian, then God's grace is still giving you a chance to avoid that ultimate judgment. Even as a non-Christian, God still continues to bless your life. But it is appointed unto men once to die, then the judgment![42]

The second evidence of God's grace is that through the Messiah, redemption for fallen humanity is made available. In Christ all the blessings of redemption, salvation, eternal life, forgiveness of sin, freedom from sin, freedom from confusion, guilt, shame, and fear are all made available. As Paul states in Ephesians 1, all the spiritual blessings in the heavenly places are offered to those who place their trust in Jesus as a free gift of God's grace!

John also makes a comment in verse 17 that seems a little strange. It seems like John is saying that there was no "grace and truth" in the law that Moses gave. But is that true? The answer to that question is both *yes* and *no*.

The law was filled with truth. It stated clearly what God expected and required of all men. But the law was cold, demanding, harsh, unyielding, and, for the most part, without mercy. To put it simply, the law demanded much.[43] But it empowered no one to accomplish its demands. As a result, the law produced guilt and shame of all kinds. The reality is that the law was a cruel taskmaster designed to drive us to realize our need for a Savior. It was designed to drive us to admit our inadequacy so we would cry out to God for mercy. That's

---

[41] Matthew 5:45
[42] Hebrews 9:27
[43] Romans 7:5–6

what makes accepting the substitutionary death of Jesus, as payment in full for all our sins so precious.

Jesus came with compassion, strength, and unlimited resources. Jesus came and provided forgiveness for our failures in observing the law. He offered to restore our relationship with God when we fell short of God's calling. But most important of all, He provided, through His grace the gift of the Holy Spirit, the power to obey the demands of the law.

The relationship between the law and Jesus is the same as the relationship between supply and demand. The law makes demands on us that are true, righteous, and just. Jesus provides the supply, the ability to meet the demands of the law. As we walk by faith, we fulfill the demands of the law.

The Only Begotten

John concludes this introduction in verse 18:

18. *No man has seen God at any time; the only begotten God, who is in the bosom of the Father, He has explained Him.*

Who is the *"only begotten God"* that John is talking about? He is, of course, the only begotten Son of God, Jesus the Messiah, that John mentions in verse 14. John is boldly proclaiming that Jesus, who eternally preexisted with the Father, is the Messiah and is the only one that has seen God the Father. Here in a nutshell is the reason the Word became flesh and dwelt among us. He came to explain God to us; to tell us God's plan for you and me, individually; to reveal God's design for man, God's will for man; and to offer you God's wonderful plan for your life. He came to pay a debt for us that, if we paid, would cost us our lives for all eternity. If we want to learn anything about God, then we must take a very close look at Jesus.

When John says, *"Glory as of the Only Begotten of the Father"* in verse 14 and again repeats in verse 18 that Jesus is *"the only begotten*

God," he means that Jesus is a reflection of the glory and character of His Father. And not only that but that Jesus is God Himself.

This to me is an amazing statement. The Old Testament is clear that no man could look upon the face of God because of His glory. But God was always able to mask that glory in different ways so He could interact with men face-to-face. He masked His glory in a burning bush when He met with Moses. The glory of God stood before Joshua in the form of a military commander to instruct him on the conquest of Jericho.

It is interesting that this is the second time the glory of God was placed in a tent. Do you remember where the glory of God was housed in the Old Testament? In a tent. Only this was a literal tent. It was called the tabernacle. God tabernacled in the midst of His people in a tent made of animal skins. The glory of God rested in the Holy of holies that traveled with the people through the wilderness. Here again, the glory of God is housed in another tent. This time, it is a tent of human flesh. In this tent of human flesh, John says, abides the *"only begotten God."*

Can you picture John and Jesus and the other disciples lying out there under the stars at night talking about this and that, commenting on the Milky Way, and noticing a falling star. As they talked together at night, gazing into the stars, it is amazing to think that they were talking with the very one who created those stars and put them up there, God Himself. Amazing!

It's hard to imagine that about Jesus, isn't it? But just like my body expresses my soul and spirit, will and emotions, so the body that housed Jesus expressed the soul, spirit, will, and intentions of the God of all creation. He was the Word in a human body made flesh.

And herein is the test of every religion or cult. What do they say about God becoming flesh and dwelling among us? Do they even recognize that Jesus was God in bodily form? John says in 1 John 4:3, *"If any man denies that Jesus Christ (Messiah) is come in the flesh, that is the spirit of anti-Christ."* What do they teach about Jesus? Was He God made flesh, or not? That's the test of heresy.

This probably explains, to some extent in verse 10, why "*the world did not know Him.*" The world Jesus stepped into was not the world He created in verse 3 in one significant way. The world Jesus stepped into had been ravaged for four thousand or so years by the havoc of sin and the fall of mankind. Man was not alone in his fall at the curse of Adam for the original sin. Nature itself fell with him.

It may also explain why, in verse 11, His own did not receive Him. They weren't looking for the guy next door. They weren't looking for some ordinary-looking man who was born in a smelly stable and was from a poor family. They weren't expecting a carpenter's son who never did anything that usually accompanied greatness. They were looking for someone of royal birth. They wanted someone more like a combination of Moses, King David, and Solomon. A leader who would vanquish Roman domination and restore the greatness of Israel.

Application

If the Word had never become flesh, you and I would have lived our entire lives in frustration, guilt, and the constant pressure of seeking without ever knowing if we are pleasing to God. The demands of the law would, to this day, keep us under a pile of doubt and guilt as we would have never been able to meet all the demands it imposed.

But thank God that He sent Jesus! In Jesus, we see the truth of what the law was really demanding of us. Through His empowering grace, He has equipped us to meet those demands. We would have never known the complete character and nature of God had not Jesus come and both showed and told us about Him. Yes, He certainly is demanding and just. But praise Him that He is equally forgiving, patient, and eternally loving. Serving Him has turned into a pleasure and is no longer a duty.

When was the last time you expressed your gratitude to the Lord for all that He has done for you? Gratitude can be expressed in more than just words. Be creative in the next several days and purposefully express your gratitude to the Lord through some actions.

CHAPTER 4

Enter the Baptizer
John 1:19-34

"Fads" in American culture have always amazed me. Do you remember the Pet Rock? After sitting in bar in Los Gatos, California, listening to people complain about their pets, Gary Dahl, who owned an advertising agency, came up with the idea of the Pet Rock. The Pet Rock came complete, in a box with breathing holes and straw in the bottom and instructions for how to care for your new pet. He sold them for $4 each. The fad lasted only six months, but in that time, Gary sold 1.5 million, making him a millionaire!

The Pet Rock was one of many. There was the Hula-Hoop, the Beanie Babies, Cabbage Patch Kids you could adopt, and on and on. Many of these still linger around, but their popularity is nothing like it was when these "oddities" first hit the market.

In the passage before us, another "oddity" has "hit the market." Like all "fads," John the Baptist's ministry had become really popular. We are told that all Jerusalem, all Judea and all the districts around the Jordan River were coming out to see him. John was both as odd in his dress as he was in his message. But his message was compelling. As many listened to him, they began confessing their sins and being baptized by John.[44] It wasn't long before the Sanhedrin, the ruling

---

[44] Matthew 3:5–6

body of Judaism consisting of seventy Pharisees, took note of what was going on.

It was not uncommon for religious "kooks" to come and go. Usually, they would arrive on the scene, and there would be an initial stir among the people. Maybe you would see some headlines in the *Jerusalem Gazette*. But after a while, they would be gone, and their small following would dissipate. We've had our share of this same phenomenon here in our country. There was Jim Jones and the Peoples Temple who moved from San Francisco to British Guiana; David Koresh in Waco, Texas; Heaven's Gate UFO religious millenarian group based out of San Diego, and the like.

John Was Different

John had begun to attract massive crowds. Not just a few hundred or even a few thousand, but multitudes. It seemed as though all of Jerusalem, Judea, and the surrounding districts had been drawn to John, and it didn't seem as though his influence was going to dissipate any time soon. In addition, his teaching and message were making a real impact on the people. It was both the message and its impact that was very bothersome for the established Jewish leadership.

John seemed to be the fulfillment of the Old Testament prophecies in both Isaiah 40:3 and Deuteronomy 18:15, 18. These prophetic passages spoke of a prophet that would arise just prior to the coming of the Messiah. John's message was radical and cut across traditional Jewish teaching. He was preaching that all a man had to do to be forgiven of their sins was to humbly confess them to God and, as a public declaration of that genuine confession to God, be baptized in water.[45]

That radically undermined the authority of the priests and temple authorities. It even posed a threat to the entire sacrificial system. It was extremely radical to think that anyone could be forgiven of

---

[45]   Mark 1:4

sin without a blood sacrifice. A large source of income for the priests came from the selling of sacrificial animals to those coming to confess their sins at the temple. John's message was not only undermining traditional Jewish teaching, but it was digging into the pocketbooks of the Jews and threatening their authority and control over the people. The Jews needed to get to the bottom of this and get there quickly!

We pick up the text in chapter 1:19–24…

19. *And this is the witness of John, when the Jews sent to him priests and Levites from Jerusalem to ask him, "Who are you?"*

20. *And he confessed, and did not deny, and he confessed, "I am not the Christ."*

21. *And they asked him, "What then? Are you Elijah?" And he said, "I am not." "Are you the Prophet?" And he answered, "No."*

22. *They said then to him, "Who are you, so that we may give an answer to those who sent us? What do you say about yourself?"*

23. *He said, "I am a voice of one crying in the wilderness, 'Make straight the way of the Lord,' as Isaiah the prophet said."*

24. *Now they had been sent from the Pharisees*

The Logical Options

We are told in verse 24 that the Sanhedrin sent priests and Levites from Jerusalem to determine *exactly* who John was. Their primary concern was to figure out the legitimacy of his ministry. One of the things that made John's ministry so impressive was that folks were willing to come all the way out into the wilderness to hear him and be baptized by him. According to verse 28, John was operating *"beyond the Jordan in Bethany."* This was Gentile territory. It was impressive that folks would travel from all over and go into Gentile territory just to hear John preach.

The Pharisees sent both priests and Levites to investigate what John was all about. The distinction between priests and Levites is a little subtle. All priests were chosen from the tribe of Levi. So, all priests were Levites. But not all Levites were priests. Priests only came from the family of Aaron, the first high priest in Israel. The priests at the temple in Jerusalem not only officiated over the religious life of the Jews, they were also rulers and judges. They were the ones that took care of the sacrifices and the operations of the temple.

The Levites who were not priests were assigned duties connected with the tabernacle.[46] They assisted the priests,[47] prepared the cereal offerings,[48] and cared for the courts and the chambers of the sanctuary among many other duties. Later, the Levites were involved in interpreting the law and thus functioned as teachers.[49] It was appropriate for the Pharisees to send those who interpreted the law, taught the law, and interacted directly with the people in the worship of God to attend to this task.

The Pharisees considered several possibilities about who John might be. Of course, the first thought was that John could be the Christ. *Christ* is a word that means "Messiah." The nation had longed for years for the coming of the Messiah. For four hundred years, there had been no prophet of God in Israel. It was as though the doors of heaven were shut and God had turned His back on them.

Then John appeared on the scene, seemingly out of nowhere. He was preaching a very unorthodox message of forgiveness. His popularity was enormous. The common folks longed for a sense of being forgiven by God. The temple ceremonies seemed to only be a temporary fix. The need to be really, completely forgiven and cleansed of sin was a compelling drive. It seemed to the priests and Levites that the only one who could be so charismatic with a "religious" message of forgiveness would be the Messiah. This Baptizer was probably the Christ.

---

[46] Numbers 3–4
[47] Numbers 1:50; 3:6, 8; 16:9
[48] 1 Chronicles 23:28–32
[49] Nehemiah 8:7, 9; 2 Chronicles 17:7–7; 35:3

John quickly and completely denied that claim, *"I am NOT the Christ."* To even be considered to be the Christ was an appalling thought to John. It is interesting that the text says John *confessed, did not deny,* and again he *"confessed"* that he was not the Christ. The Baptizer could not put the rejection of the thought that he was the Christ in stronger terms. He had even claimed to be unworthy to untie the sandals of the Christ.[50]

The second possibility that the Jews considered was that John might be Elijah. Malachi 4:5–6 prophesied that Elijah would come before the final judgment and would restore the people's relationship with God. The four hundred silent years was a clear indication to all that God was not pleased with His people. And John was all about getting people right with God. In fact, in Matthew 11:14, Jesus identifies John as the one to whom Malachi was referring. The Jews thought that Elijah would be reincarnated and do what John was doing. So maybe John was the reincarnated Elijah. It made perfect sense to them.

John's response to that was again very direct: *"I am not."* Not a whole lot of wiggle room there. One of the things I have often pondered here is why John says he is not Elijah when Jesus says in Matthew 11:14 that he was the fulfillment of the prophecy concerning Elijah. I haven't quite figured this out yet, but it may have been because John knew he wasn't a *reincarnated* Elijah. In fact, the whole concept of reincarnation is contrary to both the teachings of Judaism and Christianity. I think John recognized the similarities between his ministry and Elijah's ministry (both calling Israel to repent for sin), but his humility might not have allowed him to make such a prestigious connection.

The next possibility was that John might be the prophet. In Deuteronomy 18:15 and 18, Moses foretold that a prophet would precede the coming of the Christ as did Isaiah in Isaiah 40:3. So it made logical sense to the priests and Levites that John might be that

---

[50] Mark 1:7

prophet. Again, John does not mince words. He simply replies, *"No."* We'll discover later on in John's Gospel that, at the feeding of the five thousand, that Jesus Himself was the fulfillment of these Old Testament passages.

John's response to these inquiries reveals to us something about the character of John. As popular as he was, he was *not* about drawing attention to himself. He knew the Messiah was coming. Further, he knew he was nothing in comparison to Him. John feared taking any of the glory or credit that rightly belonged to Jesus, so he denied it all. That's a kind of humility that, in my opinion, is rare to see in those who stand behind the pulpits of our churches today.

So, Who Are You?

The Jews that came to question John were clear about their motives. They needed to report back to the Sanhedrin who John was and what he was all about. Not getting a definitive answer as to who John really was, they simply asked him in verse 22 what he had to say about himself.

From John's answer in verse 23 (where he quoted from Isaiah), it is clear that John knew not only who he was but what his mission was. John's mission was to *"make straight the way of the Lord"* or prepare the way for Jesus's arrival onto the public scene. He does so by calling attention to the fact that everyone needs to repent for their sins. Sin is the most deep-seated problem in the heart of every man. And it is one that pulls us away from God. Sin was the very reason for the past four hundred years of silence.

And you don't need a complex system of religious sacrifices, penance, or hoops to jump through in order to be forgiven of sin. You can be forgiven right here and right now. You just need to humbly, honestly, and openly confess your sin and repent before God. A heart that is repentant is a heart that is ready, clean, washed, and capable of receiving the Spirit of God that Jesus came to give. Herein lies a truism about life in any society. Any man or woman who is willing to genuinely acknowledge and humbly repent for their sin will acknowledge and embrace Jesus. Any man or woman who rejects the idea of sin and their need to repent will deny and reject Jesus. It's just the way God made you and me.

I don't want you to miss this; it is very important. In all that is usually talked about in discussing the "gospel," we usually camp on God's love and His grace in dying to save our souls. That is all true, but no man nor woman has any chance of salvation or ever experiencing God's love and mercy without first coming to the clear and resolute understanding that they are sinners that need desperately to confess their sins, openly and honestly, to God. Sin is what separates us from God. Sin was what separated Israel from God for four hundred years. There is no pathway to the grace of God without first repenting for sin. That's the issue that must be settled first.

On What Authority?

If John is nobody special like the Christ or Elijah or the prophet, then the priests and Levites have a real problem with John baptizing people for the forgiveness of sin. We continue in the text:

25. *And they asked him, and said to him, "Why then are you baptizing, if you are not the Christ, nor Elijah, nor the Prophet?"*
26. *John answered them saying, "I baptize in water, but among you stands One whom you do not know.*
27. *"It is He who comes after me, the thong of whose sandal I am not worthy to untie."*
28. *These things took place in Bethany beyond the Jordan, where John was baptizing.*

For the Jewish leadership, it seemed that if John was not a recognized authoritative figure, he should not be baptizing anyone. The priests baptized converts into Judaism because of their positions of authority. The assumption was, in order to be baptized, you needed to have some authority figure baptize you.

This was the attitude of the church in which I was raised. When I was baptized, it was done by the pastor. In fact, it *had* to be done by the pastor. Nobody else was "ordained." And if you weren't baptized by an ordained pastor, for some reason, either it didn't count, or it didn't stick!

John was a maverick. He had not been to seminary. He had not studied under Gamaliel. He was not the understudy of an approved rabbi. John had not been sanctioned by the Levitical priesthood or the Sanhedrin. He had none of the "approved" credentials necessary to be a preacher or to officiate at a baptism. John was not "ordained." The commission of priests and Levites sent out to inquire about John were saying, "If you are not someone officially sanctioned and approved, then by what authority are you baptizing?"

But where in the world in the Old or New Testaments is the requirement that you have to be a member of the ordained clergy or a priest to baptize anyone? It doesn't exist. In fact, on the day of Pentecost when three thousand folks were baptized in one day,[51] I would suggest that brother was baptizing brother. It just wasn't practically possible for the apostles to baptize three thousand in that limited amount of time.

Oh, Really

It is interesting that John doesn't answer their question. In fact, he very cleverly turns the tables on them. He questions their ability to recognize real authority. How embarrassing it must have been for these leaders of Israel when the magi came from the east, looking for the newborn king of the Jews! The magi had studied the same scriptures the Jews had. How was it possible that these men from Persia realized that the time for the birth of the Jewish Messiah had

---

[51] Acts 2:41

come, but the Jews missed it completely? Talk about being asleep at the switch! It took Godly men from a foreign country, *Gentiles*, to make them realize the time for Messiah had arrived. They should have known that.

The timing of this event (the Pharisees sending these priests and Levites out to question the Baptizer) is important here. Do you remember what Jesus did immediately after He was baptized? He went out into the desert to be tempted by the devil for forty days and nights.[52] You will note that John (the author) mentions nothing about the baptism of Jesus. The reason is that Jesus isn't baptized here. He has already been baptized. Many of these men questioning John had been at Jesus's baptism some five or more weeks earlier. They had witnessed Jesus's baptism and the Spirit descending upon Him like a dove. They had heard the Father speak out of heaven to Him.[53] That should have been a *huge* wake-up call for them, but they didn't recognize the authority of the Father in that event either. They had completely lost all understanding that real authority came from God and not from titles or positions of religious status. Who are they to question the Baptizer's authority? How arrogant!

When John says to them in verse 26, *"But among you stands One whom you do not know,"* to whom do you think he is referring? Jesus of course! I had always thought that when John said that, he was speaking in general terms. In other words, John was saying the Messiah was here today, somewhere in Israel. But John is not saying that at all. He is saying, *"Among you* stands One, right over there next to the guy in the gray tunic with the food stain under his chin, and you don't even know who He is. He is the guy with real authority, and you don't even recognize Him. You wouldn't recognize real authority if it bit you on the backside!" I am convinced that Jesus was standing right there in the crowd when the Baptizer made that statement.

---

[52] Matthew 4:1–2
[53] Mark 1:10–11

In fact, we are told in verse 29 that Jesus showed up the very next day as well and that is why, in the flow of the passage, at verse 35, the disciples follow Jesus as He leaves the crowd. The Baptizer had specifically pointed Him out as the One among the crowd. He had been there that very day the priests and Levites were questioning John.

In our current text, in verse 26, John says, *"I baptize in water."* This is a phrase that John will make three times in a very short space of time about his "commission."[54] What John was saying was that his baptism wasn't the real thing. His baptism was symbolic. It was preparatory. It was designed to get folks ready for the real thing, which would be the baptism of the Holy Spirit by Jesus.[55]

John clearly knew who he was and what his mission was. In fact, John states plainly in verse 31, *"But in order that He might be made manifest to Israel, I came baptizing in water."* He knows he is to "make manifest" (to make known; to reveal) to the nation of Israel that Jesus is the Messiah that God had promised to send ages ago. And the way he would prepare the nation of Israel to receive the Messiah when He came was to baptize folks in water as a symbolic demonstration that they had truly repented for their sins. Water symbolized the washing away or cleansing of sin. (This will be a very important concept to keep in mind when we get to Nicodemus in chapter 8.)

John also knew he was not the Messiah, Elijah, or the prophet. The very reason he acknowledged being the fulfillment of Isaiah's prophecy in verse 23 was a recognition that he was the one making the path straight for the Messiah. He was the one who was preparing the way. His emphatic statement in verse 27 that he was not even worthy to untie Jesus's sandals is a pretty humbling picture. The person whose job it was to untie the sandal was a reference to a master and a slave. When the master entered the house, his slave would stoop to untie his sandal and wash his feet. John was saying that he

---

[54] Verses 26, 31, 33
[55] Verse 33

was lower than the lowest servant when it came to any comparison to his Master, Jesus. His mission was only preparatory and symbolic.

And the point is exactly this. If you want to be baptized by the Spirit of God, which is the only way to ever experience life as God intended and designed it to be lived, *you must begin by humbly repenting of your sin*. That is how you prepare your heart for all that God desires to give you. (Again, remember this when we get to Nicodemus.)

The next day, John clearly identifies and introduces who Jesus really is:

29. *The next day he saw Jesus coming to him and said, "Behold, the Lamb of God who takes away the sin of the world!*
30. *This is He on behalf of whom I said, 'After me comes a Man who has a higher rank than I, for He existed before me.'*
31. *And I did not recognize Him, but in order that He might be manifested to Israel, I came baptizing in water."*
32. *And John bore witness saying, "I have beheld the Spirit descending as a dove out of heaven, and He remained upon Him.*
33. *"And I did not recognize Him, but He who sent me to baptize in water said to me, 'He upon whom you see the Spirit descending and remaining upon Him, this is the one who baptizes in the Holy Spirit.'*
34. *"And I have seen, and have borne witness that this is the Son of God."*

Lamb of God?

As John saw Jesus coming, he pointed to Him with his finger so all would know exactly who among the multitudes he was referring to and said, *"Behold, the Lamb of God who takes away the sin of the world."* This was a pretty amazing statement. But do the Jews listening to John get what John was saying? I'm not sure it was as clear as a bell. It seems obvious to us what John was saying. But they had a couple of problems in trying to put it together.

First of all, the term *Lamb of God* is never used in the Old Testament to identify Messiah. That was not a title or term with which they would have been familiar. In fact, the term *Lamb of God* is used only by John the Apostle and John the Baptist in the gospel of John and in the book of Revelation, which was written by John. What John the Baptizer does here is use the term as a title for Jesus and links it directly to the very purpose and mission of Jesus, as the sacrifice for sin. The association of lambs being offered as a sacrifice for sin was easy to understand. It was a common practice in the temple and as understandable as a baloney sandwich with extra mayo (which is my personal favorite kind of sandwich). The part that was a bit foggy for them was the idea that the Lamb of God (the Messiah) would be sacrificed for sin.

The other term that was a little confusing was the idea of *Lamb of God* being equated with Son of God in verse 34. Again, *Son of God* is another term that appears nowhere in the Old Testament. So, the Baptizer is using two completely unfamiliar terms, *Lamb of God* and *Son of God*. To me, this is intriguing.

I am sure the audience John was addressing, as well as the priests and Levites in particular, were able to piece things together pretty well. They were certainly familiar with all the Old Testament passages that talked about the suffering servant who would bear our stripes and heal our wounds. They understood that the Baptizer was speaking of Jesus in Messianic terms. So, they made that connection.

What John was doing is laying out the mission of the Messiah, Jesus. *Christ*, as mentioned above, means "Messiah." Later on in chapter 10, verse 24, these same Jews will ask Jesus to tell them plainly if He is the Christ or Messiah. John is saying the reason the Word became flesh was to assume the role of a sacrificial lamb, the Lamb of God's own choosing who would die on a cross for our iniquity. He would be the One who would bear our stripes, take the punishment we deserved, and give His life as a sacrifice for our sin. That's why

John now refers to Jesus in a higher sense, not just as Messiah but as the very Lamb of God who would take away the sins of the world.

The very fact that John says Jesus was the Lamb of God that would take away the sins of the world was in itself disturbing to many of the Jewish leadership. John is saying that the Lamb of God was not just taking away the sins of the Jews, but the sins of everyone in the whole world—Jews, Gentiles, and pagans of every color and stripe. And you and I can thank God for that!

Yet notice what John says in verses 31 and 33. Twice John says, *"I did not recognize Him."* Why does he say that? John, like everyone else, had real doubts about Jesus, even up until his death. Some time after John baptized Jesus, doubts crept back into John's mind. John never lived to see Jesus do any of his attesting miracles. He had been thrown into prison before that. It must have been really hard to believe the real promised Messiah had stood right before him. He knew Jesus was his cousin. He knew the miraculous events surrounding both his birth and Jesus's birth. But really, can cous' Jesus actually be the Messiah! I think John knew it in his heart, but his mind was having trouble grasping it. So God told John exactly how he would know that Jesus was the Messiah.

The sign God would give to John (so he could recognize the Messiah) was that He would be the one on whom the Spirit would descend *and remain*. The Spirit had descended on all the prophets of the Old Testament. The Spirit even descended on John as he preached repentance to the multitudes that came out to hear him.

But the Spirit never remained on any one of them. The Spirit didn't tabernacle, dwell within anyone, prior to Pentecost. The Spirit wasn't continuously available like he is with us today. The Spirit was only with them for a time until the particular mission God wanted them to accomplish was completed. Then He was gone.

But now, for the first time ever, the Spirit was going to remain on or with the Messiah, continuously. This would foreshadow how the Spirit would remain with you and me today. This was the sign John was to look for that Jesus was in fact the Son of God.

Look more carefully at John's statement in verse 32. He says, *"I have seen the Spirit descending as a dove out of heaven."* What verb tense does John use? It is a past tense, *"have seen."* When did John see the Spirit descend as a dove out of heaven upon Jesus? Clearly, at Jesus's baptism. What leads me to believe Jesus was baptized five or so weeks earlier is confirmed here in John's use of the past tense.

But notice what else John says about the Spirit in verse 32. He says that the Spirit would remain on Him. Think about that for a moment. How in the world does John know, five weeks later, that the Spirit is still remaining on Jesus? The Spirit of God is not something tangible that anyone can see. Spirit is intangible.

We aren't told exactly how John knew this. Most likely, Jesus had not done even one miracle yet. There had to be some other evidence that convinced John that the Spirit still remained on Jesus. I can only guess here, but I'll bet it had something to do with Jesus's character, mannerisms, demeanor, or behavior. We know John saw the Spirit descend on Jesus at His baptism. By some evidence, John now acknowledges that the Spirit of God continues to remain with Him.

$64,000 Question

So here is the $64,000 question. Is it obvious to people around you that the Spirit of God has descended upon you and *remains* with you? The Spirit of God has indwelt you in the exact sense that He indwelt Jesus. And John recognized the difference that the Spirit made in the character of Jesus. Do your friends recognize it in you?

They may not be able to articulate what it is about you, but it must be obvious that in some way or another that you are different. If it's not obvious, then maybe there are some sins needing to be confessed. Or maybe you need to ask God's Spirit to fill you again because you have quenched the Spirit.[56]

---

[56] 1 Thessalonians 5:19

To wrap things up, who was eligible for John's baptism? Any who were willing to confess their sins and then declare that confession publically by being baptized by John in the Jordan River. Just so no one gets confused here, John's baptism and Christian baptism are not one and the same. John's baptism was a public recognition of the confession of sin. Christian baptism goes much farther. It is also a public recognition of the confession of sin, but in addition, it is a symbolic identification with the death, burial, and resurrection of Jesus Christ.[57] Jesus was three and one-half years away from dying on a cross at this time.

And who is eligible for Jesus's baptism in the Spirit? All those who have received John's witness that Jesus is the Son of God and who have confessed their sins and, by faith, have accepted His substitutionary death as payment in full for their sins, committing their hearts and lives to Him as their Lord and Savior. To those, the Spirit of God will not only indwell but remain after the day of Pentecost.

The Baptizer concludes his testimony with the final word: *"I myself have seen and have testified that this is the Son of God."* When John says Jesus is the Son of God, he means that He is in fact God himself. John 5:18 proves that this is how the Jews understood that term. He is in fact equal in every respect to God. It is a clear claim of deity that the Jews understood. It was the reason the Jews sought to kill Jesus, for making Himself equal with God.

John the Baptist's testimony is complete. Jesus is the Messiah that had been prophesied to come for centuries. But not just the Messiah, also, as the Lamb of God who would provide the solution for the sins of the world. He would be the substitute sacrifice that the Father would offer as payment in full for the sins of all mankind. Now, in Jesus, God Himself dwells among His people in human flesh. This is the testimony of John. And this is the testimony that will get Him killed.

---

[57] Romans 6

Application

All spiritual renewal on a personal level begins with confessing sin and choosing to go in a different direction. As a personal exercise tonight, when everyone else has gone to bed, go to your "quiet place" and take a pen and tablet with you. Spend some time writing down on your tablet all the sins that come to your mind that you have committed today or even this week. After you've written them down on paper, prayerfully confess each of those sins. Then turn in your Bible to 1 John 1:9 and write that verse across your paper, right over that list of sins. Finish by thanking God for His forgiveness. Be sure to destroy this piece of paper so no one can see it. It is nobody's business but yours and God's.

CHAPTER 5

And Then They Came
John 1:35-51

Would you consider yourself a follower or a leader? If you are a follower, what kind of person would you follow? If you think about it for a moment, the world is full of followers. Rock stars, movie stars, football stars, and many, many more have multitudes of followers. Justin Bieber has won over 33.38 million followers on Twitter, narrowly beating Lady Gaga with 33.36 million, says Twitter Counter. Good grief! What is it that motivates someone to be a follower? Or what are you looking for in a leader?

In this next section of John's gospel, we run into five of the men that chose to follow Jesus and became part of His apostolic ban. John is unique in his writing about those who chose to follow the Lord. A couple of questions come almost immediately to mind. First, why does John pick these five guys to tell us about? And what are we to learn from the process that is revealed? It would not surprise me that John knew these guys before any of them were called to be followers of Jesus. We know for certain that John and his brother James were partners with Peter and Andrew in the fishing business.[58] We

---

[58] Luke 5:2ff

also know that they all lived in the same town in Galilee, Bethsaida, which was not a very big town.

Jesus's Ministry Begins

When you read the text, it seems like these first two men made some kind of spontaneous decision without giving it much thought at all. Here is how the text reads:

35. *Again the next day John was standing with two of his disciples,*
36. *and he looked upon Jesus as He walked, and said, "Behold, the Lamb of God!"*
37. *And the two disciples heard him speak, and they followed Jesus.*
38. *And Jesus turned, and beheld them following, and said to them, "What do you seek?" And they said to Him, "Rabbi (which translated means Teacher), where are You staying?"*
39. *He said to them, "Come, and you will see." They came therefore and saw where He was staying and they stayed with Him that day, for it was about the tenth hour.*

Don't let the brevity of this account fool you. The Baptizer had become a rock star in his own right by this time. As we've previously noted, thousands, even multitudes from Jerusalem, all over Judea and the surrounding districts were coming out to listen to him and be baptized by him.[59] These two men had become committed disciples of John the Baptist.[60] They believed that John's call was not only to repent personally but that the whole nation needed to repent. An atmosphere of excitement and anticipation about the coming of the Messiah had begun to spread across the land. These two had repented for their sins and been baptized by John in the Jordan River. They were earnestly looking for the Messiah to come. They knew

---

[59] Matthew 3:5
[60] John 1:35

John was the forerunner for Him and that John was preparing the way by preaching his message.

Then the day came when the Nazarene stepped forward to be baptized publically by John. It was an awkward scene. These two disciples of John were front and center when this happened. John had baptized hundreds of people, even a few of the priests.[61] John would not refuse baptism to anyone who truly repented for his or her sin.

John seemed very reluctant to baptize[62] the Nazarene. It was difficult to hear what they were saying as they stood down there in the waters of the Jordan, but John's reluctance was obvious in his body language. It was rumored that he felt unworthy to baptize the man from Nazareth. He had mentioned previously that he didn't feel worthy to even untie the thong of His sandals.[63] But the Nazarene seemed to insist. Finally, John gave in and baptized Him.

Why did Jesus go down to be baptized by John? The scriptures tell us that Jesus was sinless[64] and was the spotless Lamb of God[65]. John was baptizing those who were repenting of their sins. What sin had Jesus done that He needed to repent of? The answer is simply, none. This explains some of the reluctance of John in baptizing Jesus.

Only in Matthew's gospel are any words of Jesus recorded at His baptism, *"Permit it at this time; for in this way it is fitting for us to fulfill all righteousness." Then he* [the Baptizer] *permitted Him*[66]. You can almost hear them talking down in the water, the movement of the water against the shore muffling their conversation just a bit.

"Master, what are you doing? This is not necessary. Who am I, Lord. I am not worthy. I cannot do this thing. It is not right." John insists.

---

61 Matthew 3:6
62 Matthew 3:14
63 John 1:27
64 2 Corinthians 5:21
65 1 Peter 1:19
66 Matthew 3:15

"John," Jesus says softly, "My Father has sent you. Your mission on this earth is almost over. You have been faithful in calling all men to repent. It is necessary, as you know, that men must confess and repent of their sin in order to be capable of receiving the Spirit of our Father. You have rightly made the path straight for the ministry the Father has sent Me to accomplish. I beg you John, permit it at this time. If you will baptize Me in this way, you and I will demonstrate to all men for all time what is fitting and necessary for anyone at any time to become right with our Father. Permit it at this time, John, for in this way it is fitting for us to fulfill all righteousness. It sets the example that all men must follow."

"Yes, Lord, I will permit it." John humbly responds.

Jesus wasn't baptized because He had sinned. Jesus was baptized to affirm the ministry and message of John, that confession and repentance is the gateway of having the Spirit of God fall on you and me. It is the way to fulfill all righteousness in becoming a child of God. But let's turn our attention back to what the multitudes looking on saw.

The strangest thing happened. Everyone saw it, but describing it is quite another matter. As the Nazarene was brought up out of the water, something happened above Him. Something came out of the heavens that resembled a dove. Don't ask anyone how he or she knew exactly what was happening. No one could explain it rationally, hardly even describe it. But it seemed obvious that the Spirit of God had descended and remained upon the Nazarene!

The confirmation of that was a voice that seemed to come out of the heavens as well. Some thought they heard thunder. Others definitely thought they heard a voice. John himself said later that it was God the Father who had spoken and said that this Nazarene was His Beloved Son in whom He was well pleased. It is hard to explain. No one had ever seen anything like that before. The multitude stood in stone silence as they all looked on. The moving water against the rocks along the shore was the only other sound that could be heard.

The birds themselves seemed to be hushed. The baptism of Jesus marked the beginning of His ministry.

As the Nazarene came up out of the water, He melded back into the crowd. Then He was gone. The two followers of John continued to come out to see John as often as they could, sometimes many days in a row, hoping to see Jesus. But the Nazarene never showed up again. They had so many questions about Him. They would ask John, and John seemed to affirm that He was the Messiah. But beyond that, John didn't seem to know much about Him. All they knew was that the Nazarene was the Baptizer's younger cousin!

By the time we get to verse 35 of this chapter, Jesus had already been baptized by John. He had spent the forty days in the wilderness being tempted by the devil, and when He returned to Judea after the temptation, He must have begun His teaching ministry. Many who read the text assume that after the forty days in the wilderness, Jesus came immediately back to where John was baptizing.

Jesus must have spent some time teaching *before* He showed up in verse 36. The giveaway is that when the two disciples that followed Jesus in verse 37 are confronted by Him, they address Him with the respectful title "Rabbi." Why do they call Him *Rabbi*? "Rabbi" was a term of respect. It was what you would call a scholar or teacher, especially one who studies or teaches Jewish law. It was not just some casual greeting.

This helps us understand some of what is going on here. Jesus had already established Himself as a Rabbi. He had already been teaching. It would be my guess—and it's only a guess—that a few months must have passed since Jesus returned from the wilderness. Jesus had become known as one of the local rabbis who was teaching God's law along the Galilean shore had now come down to the same vicinity where John was preaching.

Then one day, Jesus came to see John. When John saw Him approach the crowd, John pointed directly at Him and cried out in a loud voice, "Behold! The Lamb of God who takes away the sin of the world."[67] That was a remarkable statement. John was calling Israel to repent for their sin. But this Nazarene, how could He take away the sin of the *world*? Then only a few moments later, John declared Him to be the Son of God.[68] Did John really mean that? Never once is that term, *Son of God*, used in the Old Testament as a title of Messiah; but here, the Baptizer used the term to describe One who is of the same essence with the Father. It was a remarkable claim!

The very next, day Jesus again approached John and the multitude surrounding him. This time, according to verse 35, John was speaking with two of his disciples. The Baptizer was the first to notice Him approach. For the second time, John pointed to Him and cried out in a loud voice, "Behold, the Lamb of God."[69] Again, that was not a phrase that was used in the Old Testament to describe the Messiah. But the connection with the "lamb" that God had provided Abraham as a substitute for the sacrifice of his son could not be missed.

Andrew and the Other Guy

John's affirmation of Jesus was all these two men needed. Their interest had already been piqued. Twice their mentor had referred to Him as the Lamb of God. It was as though John's declaration about Him was the sign from God they were looking for. They needed to find out more about this Nazarene. When He left this time, they decided to follow Him at some distance, not wanting to be too obvious. They just wanted to see where He was going. Maybe there would be an opportunity to ask Him some questions.

Who were these two men? John tells us that the name of one of them was Andrew down in verse 40. The other remains unnamed. It is almost universally believed that the one with Andrew was John himself, the author of the book. The rationale for that is that John never refers to himself by name in this book. He always uses oblique

---

[67] John 1:29
[68] John 1:29–34
[69] John 1:36

terms when referring to himself, like "the disciple whom Jesus loved" or the one "reclining on Jesus' breast."[70] We will discover in several places in this gospel that John was a self-effacing individual. Since he specifically names Andrew and not the other, it is most likely John himself.

It didn't take long before Jesus realized that a couple of men were following Him. Unexpectedly, He stopped and turned around to face them directly. If there would have been a bush or a rock nearby to jump behind to avoid the embarrassment of having been caught "stalking," they would have probably done that. But as it was, they were "caught!"

Jesus directly confronts the situation. *"What do you seek?"* These are the very first words of Jesus in John's gospel. His question has some unique significance. He doesn't ask *who* do you seek, but *what* do you seek. His question drives to their motivation. For me, this very first statement of our Lord in the book of John pinpoints the whole purpose of this gospel. It hits at one of the most fundamental questions facing every man and woman. What do you seek? What do you want out of life? What are you doing here? Why do you get up in the morning? What is the meaning of your life? This is perhaps the most penetrating question of our existence.

And these are the questions that this gospel will address. This is why the Word became flesh. This is why the Lamb of God takes away the sins of the world. The entire Gospel of John addressees the question "What do you seek?" for every one of us.

Andrew and John are very straightforward in their response. They weren't looking for the meaning of life; they just wanted to know where He was staying. Maybe they could come over some time and ask some questions and talk. It was clear from their response that they just wanted to get to know Him a little better.

Jesus's answer was both warm and welcoming, *"Come and see."* It was an open invitation. They were both welcomed and invited to

---

[70] John 13:23

investigate for themselves what He was all about. They could ask anything they wanted. Jesus recognized that these two men, as committed disciples of the Baptizer, would be open to the truth of who He really was. The Baptizer had opened their minds to consider who Jesus might be. But it wouldn't be until they were convinced themselves, by having all their own questions answered, that they would ever become committed followers of His. The invitation was genuine; no strings attached: "Come, see for yourself. Ask all the questions you want."

This has been the offer of the gospel since the beginning of time. Before becoming His follower, many, if not most, of us had many questions and doubts. We had questions that needed to be answered. We weren't interested in "blind faith." We needed to know some things. Everyone needs to investigate and discover for himself or herself who Jesus really is. Jesus welcomes that. No one can be forced into Christianity. The Lord realizes that the commitment of a disciple must come as the result of one's free choice after a thorough investigation.

This is what I find so weird about the Muslim jihad movement of our day. Radical Muslims pose the threat to those who are not of their faith to either convert or be killed. Are they kidding? Do they really think those "converts" that come about as the result of a death threat are real converts? Is there any better way to get a following that really hates your guts than to force someone to convert upon the threat of death? What a stupid way to make converts. I hate to be the bearer of bad news, but if a convert can't be persuaded, he or she is not a real convert.

We continue:

40. *One of the two who heard John speak, and followed Him, was Andrew, Simon Peter's brother.*
41. *He found first his own brother Simon, and said to him, "We have found the Messiah" (which translated means Christ).*

42. *He brought him to Jesus. Jesus looked at him, and said, "You are Simon the son of John; you shall be called Cephas" (which is translated Peter).*

Andrew and John were relieved at Jesus's open invitation. They apparently spent the whole day with Him,[71] and I'm sure asked Him a ton of questions. We have no idea what they talked about (I would love to have been a fly on that wall), but Andrew was convinced after spending that one day with Jesus that he was in fact the Messiah, the promised deliver of the Jews.

Along Comes Peter

After they left, Andrew immediately went to find his own brother, Peter. He couldn't wait to tell him about Jesus. But notice carefully what Andrew says to Peter. He doesn't say, "We found a guy named Jesus who claims to be the Messiah." No! He simply said, without hesitation or apology or even much explanation, *"We have found the Messiah!"* Andrew was convinced that Jesus was the "real deal" and urged Peter to come and meet Him.

Most likely John left when Andrew left. John was, no doubt, as impressed as Andrew. The record of Jesus calling these men in Mark 1 would suggest that John also went and found his brother James. Both sets of brothers—Andrew and Peter, James and John—made their living fishing on the Sea of Galilee. They beached their boats next to one another. They were already best friends.[72] All were most likely followers of the Baptizer. All were anticipating the coming of the Messiah.

I wonder what Peter really thought when Andrew told him he found the Messiah. For one thing, he must have thought that he needed to check this out for himself, so he came with his brother Andrew to meet Jesus. It seems logical to me that during the day that

[71] John 1:39 "tenth hour" could be 10:00 AM
[72] Luke 5:2–11

Andrew and John spent with Jesus, much was probably said about their brothers and their families and their work. Andrew had most likely told Jesus all about his brother, Peter, who was really the dominant one in the family. Jesus, I am sure, must have told Andrew that He would love to meet his brother.

Jesus's first reaction upon meeting Peter was to give him a new name. This seems odd at first. *Simon* means a listener, a hearer, someone who is paying attention to what is going on around him. You would think that if Simon was a "listener," that he would be contemplative, slow to speak, and thoughtful in his responses.

But we know from scriptures that Simon's character was exactly the opposite. He was impetuous, always quick to action, to speak, and to make rash judgments or promises. He had a classic case of "hoof-in-mouth" disease, talking before thinking. This was Peter's weakness. This is what made him deny Jesus three times around that charcoal fire in Caiaphas's courtyard. Andrew had told Jesus all about Peter's big mouth. Personally, I don't think there is any need to assume supernatural insight here on Jesus's part. He is simply addressing what Andrew had already told Him about his brother.

So why does Jesus give Simon the name Peter when he first walks up? First of all, to disarm Simon. He already knows that Simon is quick to make judgments. By renaming Simon, Jesus acknowledges his greatest weakness right up front. I don't think Peter was either surprised or embarrassed by this. He knew he often spoke first and thought later. Everyone knew this about Peter. He assumed Andrew would have told Jesus about him. By nicknaming him Cephas (which, translated, is Peter), Jesus shows that He already understood Peter and accepted him just like he was.

But He's telling Peter something more. With this name, Jesus was prophesying about the transformation Peter would go through as a follower of Jesus. This new name by the Rabbi was really a remarkable encouragement to Simon, and he sensed it.

This change of Peter's name by Jesus suggest a transformative change of identity that occurs in the life of every believer in Jesus. Yet it is a transformation that seems to take a lifetime for most of us to fully embrace. If you were to ask me, not that long ago, who I am, I would have said something like, "I am the son of Tom and Margaret Murray. I am Ken's younger brother. I'm the husband of Carol and the father of Mandy, Ashley, Kip and Lance. I'm a Realtor with a passion for fly fishing."

But the real answer is expressed best in the lyrics of Bill Gaither's song On the Authority,

> On the authority of the Holy Word
> I rise up and take my stand.
> I'm a blood-bought child of the living God
> Who is the great "I AM."
> I'm an heir to all that heaven hold and no principality
> Can ever take away my royal crown
> Given on His authority[73].

Yet, I am all these things. But fundamentally and most importantly, I am a child of the King.

It was John the Baptist who had initially introduced Andrew and John to Jesus. And it was Andrew who had introduced his brother, Peter, to Jesus. None of them were "followers" of Jesus quite yet. Jesus did not call them to be His disciples until *after* the Baptizer had been taken into custody (according to the other gospels).[74] But having met Him and having become convinced that Jesus was the true Messiah, the transition from John to Jesus was quickly underway.

This process by the one who knows Jesus, seeking those they love to bring them to Jesus, demonstrates the most effective pattern by which the church can most effectively grow. It is a process where those who believe reach out to those they love the most and encourage them to "come on along."

---

[73] Gaither Vocal Band from the album "I Do Believe"
[74] Matthew 4:12, 18–19; Mark 1:14–17

Philip and Nathanael

John continues:

43. *The next day He purposed to go forth into Galilee, and He found Philip. And Jesus said to him, "Follow me."*
44. *Now Philip was from Bethsaida, of the city of Andrew and Peter.*
45. *Philip found Nathanael and said to him, "We have found Him of whom Moses in the Law and also the Prophets wrote, Jesus of Nazareth, the son of Joseph."*
46. *And Nathanael said to him, "Can any good thing come out of Nazareth?" Philip said to him, "Come and see."*
47. *Jesus saw Nathanael coming to Him, and said of him, "Behold, an Israelite indeed, in whom is no guile!"*
48. *Nathanael said to Him, "How do You know me?" Jesus answered and said to him, "Before Philip called you, when you were under the fig tree, I saw you."*
49. *Nathanael answered Him, "Rabbi, You are the Son of God You are the King of Israel."*
50. *Jesus answered and said to him, "Because I said to you that I saw you under the fig tree, do you believe? You shall see greater things than these."*
51. *And He said to Him, "Truly, truly, I say to you, you shall see the heavens opened, and the angels of God ascending and descending on the Son of Man."*

The next disciple Jesus "recruits" seems very purposeful. The following day, Jesus deliberately headed for Galilee. Galilee was some sixty miles to the north, at least a three-day walk. According to verse 43, it was there He found Philip. This was His purpose for going to Galilee. Jesus made a special appointment just to find Philip!

Philip, according to verse 44, was from Bethsaida. We are told that this was the same city that Andrew and Peter were from. Being from the same town, the likelihood is great that they all knew each other. The town wasn't that big. This brings up an interesting question. Why didn't Andrew or John find Philip and bring him to Jesus?

We don't really know. Maybe they didn't think Philip was a likely candidate. Maybe they didn't think Philip would be interested. Perhaps they didn't know Philip all that well. We know almost nothing about Philip from the gospels. The other gospel writers all but ignore him. Only here in John's gospel do we have a record of Jesus calling him to be a follower, but we know from Acts that once Jesus got hold of Philip, his life turned around. Philip eventually became one of the greatest evangelists (second only to Paul) in the book of Acts. It was Philip that opened the door of the gospel to the Samaritans.

The calling of Philip in John's gospel, although brief, is revealing. Jesus simply says, *"Follow me,"* and Philip seems to drop everything to follow Him. Really? Does that make any logical sense at all? Are we to suppose that Philip had never met, seen, or heard of Jesus before and, because of two words, drops everything and follows a complete stranger? I think not!

In John's gospel, the Baptizer is still involved in his ministry along the Jordan as late as chapter 4:1–2. John doesn't record the arrest of the Baptizer. And we know, as previously discussed, that the call of Andrew, Peter, James, and John to follow Jesus doesn't take place until *after* the Baptizer is arrested.

All this drives the question, "When did Jesus go into Galilee to find Philip?" It seems to me that John inserts this paragraph here to include the call of Philip and Nathanael, but the chronology may have been after the arrest of the Baptizer in chapter 4. If this is true, a couple of things make a lot more sense.

According to Matthews's gospel, Jesus had already settled in Capernaum in Galilee.[75] According to Mark's gospel, He had already begun to preach along the shores of the Sea of Galilee.[76]

---

[75] Matthew 4:12–13,18
[76] Mark 1:14–15

According to Luke's gospel, Jesus had already become fairly well known by this time.[77]

Here is my point. This was not the first encounter by Jesus with Philip or any of these men. They had all heard Him teach on several occasions. They had heard Him in the synagogue in Capernaum. They had heard Him on the beach along the seashore. And what Jesus had been saying and teaching made an abundance of sense to Philip.

When Jesus purposed to go forth into Galilee to find Philip, it was because He had had His eye on Philip previously. There is nothing in the text to lead us to assume Jesus had never seen Philip before. In fact, the text would indicate quite the opposite. He had noticed Philip in the crowd on previous occasions. Likewise, when Jesus told Nathanael that He had seen him under a fig tree, before Philip talked to him, it could very well have been because Jesus had actually seen Nathanael under a fig tree on more than one occasion. In addition, Jesus had previously observed Nathanael's response to His teaching and knew he was a man that had no guile.

The calling of these men isn't "out of the blue" where they just respond like some kind of robots. There is history here. John's record is brief and to the point. He simply doesn't fill in all the blanks. When Jesus says to Philip, "Follow me," Philip had been hoping for some time that the Rabbi would ask him to be His follower. Philip had already made up his mind about following Jesus before he was asked. He had already become convinced by Jesus's teaching that He was the Messiah of God.

The text tells us that Jesus purposely went to Galilee to find Philip and called him to be His disciple. Most believers can remember a time when they accepted Jesus as their Lord and Savior. We think we found Christ. But the reality is, and I believe will become abundantly apparent when we see Him face-to-face, that it was He who purposed to go forth into Spokane, San Jose, New York or

---

[77] Luke 4:14–16

wherever it was and He found you! He called you by name and you became His follower. I thank Him every day He found me!

Philip next goes and finds Nathanael. Nathanael is the one the other gospel writers call Bartholomew. Bartholomew is Nathanael's patronym—the name of his father. Nathanael's real name is Nathanael Bartholomew. Unlike Andrew, Philip doesn't simply describe Jesus as the Messiah to Nathanael. Instead, Philip goes into much more detail. Philip tells him that Jesus was the one about whom Moses and the prophets wrote. Philip was no dummy. He knew his Bible, and he believed what the prophets had said about the coming Messiah. Philip based his appeal to Nathanael on the scriptures. Clearly, Nathanael wasn't a man to be taken in by the many false Messiahs of the day.

Nathanael is obviously a skeptic by nature. He doubts that Messiah would come out of Nazareth, and Nathanael's comment is well taken. There is no reference to Nazareth anywhere in the Old Testament. Besides, Nazareth was not much more than a frontier town that had sprung up because of the intersection of a couple of trade routes. It was small and somewhat rural. Nazarenes were not necessarily considered sophisticated or even very educated. There was a Roman garrison there that controlled that area of Galilee and was therefore an area despised by the Jews. Matthew's comment in Matthew 2:23, "He shall be called a Nazarene," is difficult to understand. That quote cannot be found in the Old Testament! It could be that Matthew is addressing the fact that Messiah would be despised and rejected as Nazarenes were despised and rejected by the elite of Judaism.

Nathanael wondered if Messiah would come from such a lowly place as Nazareth. Today, you would consider Nathanael as not being politically correct. You might even consider him to be a racist. When Philip told Nathanael that Jesus was a Nazarene, Nathanael judged Jesus on basis of his background.

But Jesus had a judgment about Nathanael too. Without hesitation, like with Peter, Jesus commented directly on the content of Nathanael's character as he approached. Jesus had observed that Nathanael was a straightforward, honest man. He affirmed to Nathanael that he was a man who was honest to a fault. He spoke his mind openly. Nathanael may not have been full of grace and truth, but he was definitely full of truth, for the most part. Again, I don't think this is some kind of supernatural insight. It comes from common sense by having observed Nathanael before on several occasions.

Jesus's response hit a cord with Nathanael. When Nathanael asked how Jesus knew about him in verse 48, Jesus responded that He had previously taken notice of him under a fig tree. Nathanael's response seems extreme, like he's jumping to a conclusion about Jesus. But John doesn't give us the whole conversation that went on here. The point the Spirit of God wants us to get out of this dialogue between Jesus and Nathanael is that Nathanael had become thoroughly convinced that Jesus was in fact the real, promised Messiah. Which was exactly the same conclusion Andrew, John, and Peter had come to after their encounter with Jesus. Clearly, from my point of view, Nathanael was looking for and anticipating the coming of the Messiah as well.

The two terms Nathanael used to describe Jesus are *Son of God* and *King of Israel*. One speaks of His relationship with the Father, the other of His relationship with Israel, the nation. This is clear evidence that Jesus's subsequent use of the term *Son of God* was not something unexpected or strange in the ears of the Jews. All were looking for the coming of the Son of God, the true King of Israel.

Jesus was equally shocked at the depth of Nathanael's understanding and acceptance. The fact that the Son of God, the King of Israel, had taken notice of Nathanael under the fig tree had impressed him deeply. Nathanael was willing to follow without question.

Jesus's response to Nathanael's acceptance in verse 51 challenged him even further. In effect, Jesus said, "You haven't seen anything yet!" Jesus's referenced the dream of Joseph when he was fleeing Esau. Here, Jesus gives Nathanael an insight into His mission. The dream speaks of a mediator between God and Man, One who both represents God to men and men to God. This is why the Word became flesh and dwelt among us. Jesus's whole mission on earth was to reveal the nature and character of God to men. Jesus was the revelation of the plan and will of God for every man. Jesus represented *God to man*.

Eventually, through His sacrifice as our Savior, He will present every one of us who believe to the Father as those whose sins have been paid in full. He is our mediator. He will represent *men to God*.

The proof of all this will be evident in the last days. Nathanael and every one of us who have believed and accepted His sacrifice on our behalf will see Him in His glory. We will see the angels of heaven both ascending and descending with Him when He comes again.

Application

John's record of the introduction of these five men to Jesus is extremely varied. Andrew was the compliant follower of the Baptizer who was ready to accept the Messiah. John was the quiet, "tag-along" who hid somewhat in the shadow of Andrew, but who was equally committed. Peter was the impetuous, brash believer who needed to learn how to "be quick to hear and slow to speak." Philip was waiting, hoping, wishing the Master would call, and didn't hesitate to come when that happened. Nathanael was the skeptical, thoughtful, curious one. When shown the truth, he responded completely and immediately.

This is just a sample that John gives us of those who become followers of Jesus. The encouragement to us is that we not make judgments on who we think is or is not a potential follower. Like Andrew and John, our job is to seek out those we love the most. Jesus is completely capable to seek out those He knows have expressed interest.

All are welcome—questions, doubts, and all. Like this variety of men who become followers of Jesus, He accepts every one of us—lumps, bumps, warts, and bruises. Jesus welcomes an honest investigation. Jesus never asks anyone to change before they become His follower. He takes us "as is" and will affect the change He desires from the inside out.

We will see throughout this gospel that many will question Jesus. Many, particularly the Jewish leadership, will question Him with evil intent. They will question Him with the intent to discredit Him because they have no interest in ever becoming a follower. That motivation never works. If the intent is not genuine, wanting to understand and discover the truth about who Jesus is will never happen.

These men are not college professors, political elites, business professionals, the wealthy or influential, or any of those most of us would consider "important" people. Don't misunderstand me. I am not in any way implying that "important" people aren't welcome. They certainly are. It's just that Jesus isn't seeking any particular class. He did not come just for the elite, nor did He come just for the poor. He came seeking all who genuinely want to know the truth. Is that you?

If it is you, is there anyone in your sphere of influence that might join you in becoming a follower of Jesus? Think of one name, just one. Pray about that person this week. Pray particularly that the Lord would open some kind of opportunity to share your faith with them.

CHAPTER 6

Just Another Wedding
John 2:1-12

Do you like to go to weddings? I do, but they definitely have some drawbacks. For one, you have to get all dressed up. You know—coat, tie, polished shoes, pressed slacks, etc. Being raised in Planada, California (yes, it does exist), as a kid, dressing up has always been quite a bother. Then there are the crowds at a wedding. Crowds have never been my thing either. I don't do well with "chitchat." My wife has perfected the art, enjoys it, and does very well in a crowd. I usually look for a seat in a corner so I can just watch. People watch, that's what I do well in a crowd!

When I go to weddings, I often think of Jesus going to the wedding in Cana of Galilee and wonder if He really liked it. I'm sure He did, at least more than I do. In the text before us, Jesus attends a wedding in Cana. Do you think He got all dressed up? Hmmm? We pick up the text in chapter 2:

1. *On the third day there was a wedding in Cana of Galilee, and the mother of Jesus was there;*
2. *and both Jesus and His disciples were invited to the wedding.*

The Wedding

When we consider the wedding in Cana that Jesus went to, we must dismiss everything we currently think of as a wedding in the twenty-first century. There was no wedding party standing up front in a church or synagogue. There was no bride walking down the aisle. There were no "wedding vows" or "I do" statements. In fact, there was no ceremony at all. Even in Jewish weddings with the canopy, the vows before the priest, the breaking of the glass, all of that was developed centuries after the death and resurrection of Jesus.

In Jesus's day, weddings were quite different. There were three parts to a wedding.[78] The first stage was the contract. A legally binding contract was signed between the father of the bride and the bridegroom, long before the marriage was ever consummated. With the contract came the promise of a dowry or bride price. It could take years before the groom could save enough money to pay the bride price. Joseph worked seven years for free to pay for Rachel before Laban pulled the "switch" on him and he got Leah as a wife instead of Rachel.[79] He then worked another seven years free labor for Rachel before she became his bride.[80] The bride may or may not even know who her husband will be, but the couple was considered legally married once the contract was signed.

The groom kept a copy of the contract, the father of the bride kept a copy, and a copy was filed with the local synagogue. There was no sex, no living together, not even any dating as we know it. This was done by the father of the bride to protect his daughter and ensure that she had a good husband. The contract, once signed, was legally binding. They were married. It was called "betrothed," but they were as married as they would ever be.[81] It took a legal act of

---

[78] http://www.bible.ca/marriage/ancient-jewish-three-stage-weddings-and-marriage-customs-ceremony-in-the-bible.htm

[79] Gen. 29:18–25

[80] Gen. 29:27–30

[81] Matt. 1:18

divorce to undo the contract even though the couple may have never even met before.

The second stage of the wedding was the consummation. Once the dowry was paid, the groom was invited to the home of the bride, and a room was set aside for the couple to consummate the union in the home of the bride. It would seem in Joseph's case with Leah that he was so drunk he didn't know who he went to bed with that night.[82]

After the union was consummated came the third stage of the wedding. The bride and the groom, along with the bridesmaids and groomsmen, walked in a procession to the groom's house where the celebration took place. The celebration would typically last a week. This was typically an open invitation to the whole community. It was when Joseph woke up the next morning that he discovered whom he had had sex with. By that time, the "knot" had been tied. He was stuck.

Everyone was invited to celebrate the union of the new couple. There was typically a lot of eating and a lot of drinking. That was a wedding in Jesus's day. There was no ceremony, no walking down an aisle, no vows, no canopy, no broom, no breaking of a glass, nothing we typically think of today. It was to this third stage, the celebration, that Jesus and his new disciples were invited. It was there they met Jesus's mother, Mary, who was also an invited guest.

The text tells us this was on the third day. Is there significance to that? Maybe yes and maybe no. We last left Jesus in Bethany near the Jordan River where John was baptizing. Apparently, Jesus was aware of the wedding, and after meeting the initial disciples, Andrew and John, they all head "home" to Galilee for the wedding. It was a sixty-mile walk that normally took three days. So, on the third day after leaving Bethany, Jesus showed up at the wedding in Cana of Galilee with His disciples. However, I do believe there is a deeper significance to the third day that we will see in a moment.

---

[82] Gen. 29:21–23

A Mother's Concern

In John's brief account of what happened at this wedding, he focuses on a concern that the mother of Jesus had during the celebration:

3. *When the wine ran out, the mother of Jesus said to Him, "They have no wine."*
4. *And Jesus said to her, "Woman, what do I have to do with you? My hour has not yet come."*
5. *His mother said to the servants, "Whatever He says to you, do it."*

It would seem that Mary is concerned with the lack of wine. But I don't think that is actually the case. It's not that the lack of wine for the long celebration isn't a concern. It seems to me that that would be more the wine steward's concern than it was Mary's.

I think Mary's real concern ran a little deeper. Here (and this is only my opinion), Mary sees a great opportunity for her Son. Consider for a moment what insights Mary had into the life of Jesus that no one else had. She had never gotten over her miraculous pregnancy and the birth of her firstborn. I don't think any woman would ever get over an immaculate conception!

She knew Jesus was special. The angel told her He would be great (that hadn't happened yet!), He would be called the Son of the Most High (not yet!), that the Lord God would give Him the throne of David (well, it's getting kind of late for that; he's already thirty years old and no throne was in sight!), that He would reign over the house of Jacob (that hadn't happened, that she could tell), that His kingdom would have no end (as far as Mary could tell, it didn't seem to even have had a beginning), and that nothing would be impossible with God (and God was right—nothing was happening).

Then there were the magi who came from the east to Bethlehem to worship Him, bring valuable gifts of gold, frankincense, and mirth.

She recalled that the angel of God had told her husband, Joseph, to take the family and flee to Egypt. That spared her baby son's life as Herod ordered the murder of all those innocent babies around Bethlehem shortly after they left the area.

Then finally, some thirty years later, cousin John had stepped forward, opening some real doors for Mary's Son. Jesus had just been baptized a couple of months earlier, and what a great event that was. The Spirit of God actually descended upon Him and remained with Him. John had declared that He was the Son of God, the Messiah.

And what has He been doing since then? Nothing! Goofing around, collecting a bunch of new friends. "My goodness," Mary thinks. "Will He ever amount to anything? His potential is being wasted. He's got to begin doing what the angel said He would do."

A Divine Opportunity

Here is a divine opportunity from Mary's point of view. This is a large wedding (we'll see how large in a moment). All their friends were there. Everyone important in town was there. This was the perfect time and place for Jesus to launch His ministry and get on with it. He's got so much to accomplish and so little time to get it all done. This is a golden opportunity.

The wine was running out at the celebration. What a faux-pas that would be! Mary remembered that the angel had told her that nothing was impossible with God. Jesus can somehow fix this problem of no wine and, in so doing, begin to establish His ministry. *Let's do this thing*—that was Mary's real concern, not the lack of wine.

Jesus had never done a miracle up to this point. Is Mary asking Him to perform a miracle? Mary doesn't fully understand what she is asking Him to do. One gets the feeling from the text that Mary thinks Jesus needs to "get on" with His ministry. So, by asking Him to do something about the lack of wine, maybe He can bring some attention to Himself. Mary seems to think that is a good thing. He could use some attention in order to get on with fulfilling all that the angel told her about Him so long ago. It really isn't much more complicated than that.

Jesus's response to Mary seems really harsh. If you don't mind, head down a rabbit trail with me for a moment. I want you to put on your "parent hat" and use a little "divine" imagination. Have you ever had a "heart-to-heart" talk with your son or daughter about some important issue? Most of us have at different times. (At our house, we called them Shari's talks. Shari's was a local restaurant where I would take the kids for a serious talk. Serious talks seemed to go down better with hot-chocolate.)

Do you think Mary ever had a "heart-to-heart" talk with Jesus about His birth and her encounter with Gabriel? Of course she did. It's inconceivable that she would have never asked Him about those things. We know she constantly pondered them in her heart. So how did those conversations with Jesus go? I can easily imagine, when Jesus was twenty-eight years old, He and Mary were taking a walk together and talking, alone, just the two of them. The conversation may have gone something like this:

"Son, you know Joseph isn't your real father, don't you?"

"Yes, Mom, I know," Jesus replies.

"Are you really going to sit on the throne of King David like the angel said?" Mary asks.

"Yes, Mom. In time," Jesus replies again.

"And I suppose you will rule over the house of Jacob, all twelve tribes?" Mary further inquires.

"You'll understand that when the time comes, Mom," Jesus says.

"I know you are special, Son, because of how you were born. But the angel Gabriel, who appeared to me, told me you were the Son of the Most High. Does that just mean you are special, or does it mean more? I know we are all sons and daughters of God," Mary ponders.

"I know this sounds crazy, Mom, but I'm really your son. I am a man, just like Dad and my brother James. But I am God too. I am the exact representation of my real Father in heaven. I know that is hard to understand. But one day, that too will be clear to you," Jesus explains.

"Then, can you really do miracles?" Mary asks.

"Mom, I can do anything the Father asks me to do. No more and no less," is Jesus's answer.

Can't you hear that conversation? The one thing Mary clearly remembered the angel saying is, *"Nothing would be impossible with God."* So here is the golden opportunity for her Son to so something to get His ministry off the ground.

A Rebuke?

Mary had brought the problem of the wine giving out to her son, Jesus. Jesus's response sounds startling, *"Woman, what have I do to with you?"* The Hebrew idiom is actually, "What to me and to you?" Note that Jesus address His mom as *Woman* and not as *Mom.* This is a very important observation. We'll see Jesus use this same term again with His mom from the cross at the end of this gospel.

This is not disrespectful. By using the term *woman,* Jesus is showing respect to his mom. It is how He would address any woman. The reason He does this is because He is not addressing her as her son but as her Lord, as her Master, as the Messiah. There is no question in my mind that Mary picked up on that immediately. I believe that is clear in her response to the servants who were with her when she tells them, *"Whatever He says, do it."* That is Mary's expression of trust and faith in Him as her Lord.

In the idiomatic phrase Jesus uses, He is telling Mary that she really doesn't understand what she is asking. Jesus is not saying he will not do anything, because he does do something. He knows that she is trying to be helpful. He knows that she is trying to get Him to launch His ministry. And He knows that she knows that He can fix this wine problem, if it was the Father's will.

But He is telling her that what He will do will not accomplish what she expects. Mary wants Jesus to call attention to Himself in order to launch His ministry among men. Mary wasn't sure why Jesus was "hiding" His true potential.

But Jesus never did anything motivated by calling attention to Himself. His sole motivation was to call attention to the Father. Mary didn't realize that Jesus had already started His ministry. He had already begun to build the base of disciples that He would train over the next three years. These would be the men that would carry on what He would begin. Mary had no idea of what the Father was already doing through her Son.

I don't even think Mary had any idea that Jesus would turn water to wine either. Because of the awakening of Mary's expectations, due to the events at the Jordan River, Mary was assuming that Jesus would use this opportunity to announce or demonstrate his true calling as Messiah. That seems evident from Jesus's comment, *"My hour has not yet come."*

Like Sarah with Abraham, Mary is pushing things along too much, and she's pushing in the wrong direction. The truth of the matter is, there never will be a public announcement or a "coming-out party" for Jesus to announce His Messiahship. It will soon enough become evident just through the demonstration of His life. It's interesting to note that doing the miracle of turning the water to wine had almost no effect. There was confusion as to why the best wine was saved to the last. Certainly, the stewards who carried the water realized what happened, as well as Jesus's disciples. But from the text, it doesn't appear that Jesus gained any notoriety from it. From Mary's point of view, this didn't accomplish what she really hoped it would. Good intentions are never a good justification for doing things the wrong way.

When Jesus told Mary, *"My hour has not yet come"*, He was telling her that the Father was the one that was in control of His timing. Just a "sidebar" comment here. Mary suffered the same malady most of us suffer. Mary seemed to assume Jesus should operate on her timetable. Mary thought she knew when and how Jesus should announce His ministry. Mary was tired of waiting. The baptism was over. John the Baptist had straightened the path. Jesus had already chosen some disciples. *My goodness, young man, get on with it. Time was a-wasting.*

Isn't that so "human?" All of us clearly understand the fact that we know much better than God when He should come to our aid. So, why does He linger? What is He waiting for? What sense does it make for ISIS to slaughter innocent Christians when He could stop it? Good grief, God. DO SOMETHING! Isn't that exactly how we think?

Let's move on:

6. *Now there were six stone waterpots set there for the Jewish custom of purification, containing twenty or thirty gallons each.*
7. *Jesus said to them, "Fill the waterpots with water." So they filled them up to the brim.*
8. *And He said to them, "Draw some out now and take it to the headwaiter." So they took it to him.*
9. *When the headwaiter tasted the water which had become wine, and did not know where it came from (but the servants who had drawn the water knew), the headwaiter called the bridegroom,*
10. *and said to him, "Every man serves the good wine first, and when the people have drunk freely, then he serves the poorer wine; but you have kept the good wine until now."*

Stone Pots and Good Wine

I thought wine came in wineskins. I'm pretty sure wine didn't come in stone pots, but what were these stone pots Jesus used? They were the pots that held the water that was used to wash the feet of the guests as they entered the groom's home. The text tells us there were six pots holding 20 to 30 gallons of water each; that's 120 to 180 gallons of water. I'll bet it wouldn't take much more than one-half gallon of water to wash anyone's feet or a gallon at most. This wedding was probably 150 to 180 folks in attendance.

Jesus had the servants Mary brought with her fill the pots to the "brim." That would give us almost 180 gallons of water. That is going to translate into 180 gallons of wine. That's a pretty big frat party according to anyone's standard.

The fact that the pots that Jesus used were generally used to wash dirty feet has some real symbolic significance. Who would ever put good wine, excellent wine, in a pot that was used to wash dirty feet? That is quite a contrast.

These pots were used for the most menial task. This wasn't fine pottery. This wasn't Waterford Crystal. This wasn't special order pots from the Pottery Barn. These are just common, ordinary, run-of-the-mill pots you would get on sale at Walmart. Yet they are being used by Jesus for the very best wine ever to cross the lips of a man.

The Apostle Paul later likens us to clay pots. Paul's imagery is not unlike the imagery Jesus uses here. As clay pots, we will be filled with a treasure of unspeakable worth, Paul says. Here is an illustration of ordinary pots being filled with the most valuable treasure of the wedding. Perhaps this is a picture of the mission and ministry of the Messiah, and maybe this is why this event took place on the third day as verse 1 says.

When exactly did the water become wine? We don't know with certainty. Maybe immediately when the pots were filled. Maybe when the waiter took some out. It doesn't seem likely that the waiter would take a cup of water to the headwaiter without tasting it first. Or maybe when the headwaiter took a sip, the water instantly became wine.

It seems clear to me that the stewards must have tasted the wine before daring to take it to the headwaiter. They knew the water had already turned to wine, and it was a good wine, indeed. A good wine has a fragrant aroma that the stewards must have noticed (or so I have been told).

For all you legalists, this was *real* wine, fermented grape juice. The kind you can get drunk on. There is no prohibition of drinking wine anywhere in the Bible (except for the Nazarite vow).[83] Paul even

---

[83] Num. 6:2–3

encourages Timothy to drink a little wine to settle his stomach.[84] It is ludicrous to think that any Jewish wedding would be celebrated without some good wine. It was customary.

It is important to notice that Jesus did this miracle without a prayer, without a word of command, with no hysterical shouting, no pleadings to God with a contorted face, no laying on of hands, no binding of Satan, no hocus-pocus, no mumbo-jumbo, nothing. He didn't even touch the water or taste it to see if it had really turned to wine.

He did it with quiet dignity, with simplicity and with effectiveness. In fact, He doesn't even seem to stand around to take credit for it. That is exactly how He filled you and me with the Holy Spirit. There was no fanfare, no lightning strikes, no thunder clapping, no loud shouts and hallelujahs or loud demonstrations. The very Spirit of God just simply, quietly, with profound dignity filled your heart to the brim. The old water that filled you became new wine. You knew immediately there was a difference. The difference was quietly but definitively revealed to you. That is what is pictured here. This is how Jesus will baptize you with His Holy Spirit.

On a different plane, what happened here was a miracle that shortcut the natural process. This was a miracle of nature. Water naturally turns to wine in nature. Rain falls out of the sky in droplets of water, grape vines soak up that moisture, the water droplets fill the grapes as they ripen, the grapes are then crushed to release the moisture, and the moisture then naturally ferments. That is how wine is made, naturally.

Jesus simply shortcuts the process in an instant. He is the very one who John says in 1:3 *"made all things come into being."* He is the God of all of the created order and the Messiah of nature itself. Just as He transformed the natural order of wine in an instant, His intent is to change human nature into divine nature in an instant as well, through faith.

---

[84] 1 Tim. 5:23

Verse 10 gives us some insight about the time frame of this wedding. The party has been going on for a while, maybe even two or three days. Like I mentioned earlier, the celebration portion of the wedding could last a week. The fact that they had run out of wine is another indicator of that. All the good wine had run out. In fact, all the bad wine that followed the good wine had run out. So folks had already drunk freely. We are late into the wedding celebration at this time.

The headwaiter's statement, *"Every man serves the good wine first, and when men have drunk freely, then that which is poorer"* means exactly what it implies. This wine isn't grape juice. It's fermented grape juice wine. It's the kind of wine that when folks drink it freely, they get drunk or tipsy (*drink feely* means "have become drunk"). At a minimum, they lose their ability to discern good wine from bad wine.

First Miracle

11. *This beginning of His signs Jesus did in Cana of Galilee, and manifested His glory, and His disciples believed in Him.*
12. *After this He went down to Capernaum, He and His mother and His brothers and His disciples; and they stayed there a few days.*

John tells us that this was the first of the miracles that Jesus did. There are seven major miracles recorded in the book of John. "Signs" were not just miracles, but miracles that pointed to some greater truth. Jesus's miracles (like this one) were designed to attest to the fact that Jesus was one with the Father. They were the proof, as the Old Testament declared, that Jesus was really the Messiah the prophets had foretold would come. He was the reflection of the nature and character of God the Father. With this first miracle, Jesus is establishing the fact that of primary importance, He is indeed the God of all creation. He made it, it is His, and He can use it as He pleases.

That impact was not lost on the disciples. They believed in him. (A note of caution here. They believed he was the Messiah, but what that meant to them is not necessarily clear yet. They may have understood the title, but they clearly haven't understood His mission yet.)

After the wedding, the family and the disciples return to Capernaum. For many (mostly Catholics), the Virgin Mary remained a virgin until she died. But Jesus clearly had brothers and sisters. Blood brothers is the intended meaning in verse 12, since disciples are specifically mentioned as a separate class. Mary and Joseph had children after Jesus was born. Jesus had both half-brothers and half-sisters. In Acts 9, James, Jesus's half-brother, is identified as the head of the Jerusalem church. He is also the author of the book of James in the New Testament. And this same James, the half-brother of Jesus, wasn't even a believer until after Jesus's crucifixion and resurrection.

Application

The reason John pens this account seems obvious to me. Here Jesus sets the bar on the ministry that is to follow. The whole reason God became man in the flesh was to fill the stone-cold pots of humanity with the sweet wine of His Holy Spirit. God delights in taking that which is ordinary, bland, and mundane (you and me) and *putting into it* something that is rich with flavor and fragrance that brings joy and delight to others.

That is exactly what God desires to do for you and me, if we, like the disciples, will simply believe in Him. And he will do it instantaneously, quietly, with dignity, and without fanfare or human intervention. God takes what is simple and makes it simply amazing. Purposely ask Him to express His amazing power through you as you go into some specific meeting or appointment this week.

CHAPTER 7

The Mother of All House Cleanings

John 2:13-25

Have you ever been in a situation that was so embarrassing that you wished you could crawl into a hole and hide where no one could see or find you? I've had more than my share of these uneasy experiences.

I'll never forget the time back in the early '70s when I got up to preach a sermon on Sunday morning. I was the college/high school pastor and got very few opportunities to stand before the entire congregation. The teaching pastor had gone on vacation for a couple of weeks, and the elder board asked if I would fill in.

I was both eager and intimidated by the opportunity, but took it. I realize today, in this modern age of being "seeker friendly," things in the "Bible Church" and "nondenominational church" communities have become pretty casual. Hardly anyone anymore wears a coat and tie to church, and a suit and tie is very rare, even with the teaching pastor. Everyone is trying to fit in and make folks feel as comfortable as possible. It's an attempt to minimize the perceived clergy/laity barrier. I have no problem at all and am comfortable with this approach. I'm just making the observation.

However, back in the early '70s, I came to church dressed appropriately with a coat, tie, dress slacks, and polished shoes. My wife made sure everything matched. I was dressed to the "nines." My faithful and supportive wife, along with our small children, was dutifully sitting in the front row. The congregation was about 350 folks.

At the appropriate time in the service, I came up onto the platform to teach God's Word. I never liked pulpits. I've always felt that they presented a kind of mental/psychological barrier between the preacher and the congregation. So I stood in front of the pulpit, as close to the congregation as I could. In fact, I would often step down among the aisles of the congregation. I just felt it made for a better connection between speaker and audience. I got that planted in my head when I was a "speech communication" major at San Jose State University.

As I began my opening dialogue, I noticed Carol, my wife, frantically trying to say something to me from the front row. She was not talking aloud but was moving her lips dramatically trying to get me to read her lips. I continued for a bit, struggling between keeping on track with my sermon and trying to read her lips. But I couldn't do it. I knew whatever she had to say was important, and I couldn't understand her.

So I stopped what I was saying, excused myself from the audience, stepped over toward Carol, and said to her in a quiet voice (with the mic clipped to my lapel still on), "What is it?" She said as quietly and discreetly as she could (with my mic still on!), "You're unzipped!"

The crowd laughter was spontaneous, almost a knee-jerk reaction. I looked down. She was right! "Excuse me," I said, and turned around to zip up. It was probably the most effective "icebreaker" I've ever done. But even the Lord couldn't have made a hole big enough for me to crawl into at that moment! Recovery was near impossible.

Just Another Passover

What happens next in our text is one of those monumental embarrassing events for the disciples of Jesus. It is the cleansing of the temple in Jerusalem. This is the first recorded Passover in John's gospel. Passover was one of the three major festivals required for all Jews who were capable of attending. Jerusalem had swollen to several times its normal size during this festival. Jews from all over the empire had crowded into every nook and cranny available for housing. Large tent camps were set up around the city to house the overflow. This was a major event in the life of any Jew. Navigating through the temple during Passover was worse than Disneyland on a holiday weekend.

The text begins like this:

13. *The Passover of the Jews was near, and Jesus went up to Jerusalem.*
14. *And He found in the temple those who were selling oxen and sheep and doves, and the money changers seated at their tables.*
15. *And He made a scourge of cords, and drove them all out of the temple, with the sheep and the oxen; and He poured out the coins of the money changers and overturned their tables;*
16. *and to those who were selling the doves He said, "Take these things away; stop making My Father's house a place of business."*

John's description of this event is very simple and straightforward. However, it was anything but a simple, straightforward scene. I want you to visualize with me exactly how this scene went down. The first century media, the *Jerusalem Times* (if they would have had one), would have run the headline in the evening press, "A Terrorist Attack on Holy Ground!" The opposing *Palestine Post* runs with the headline, "Radical Rabbi Runs Amok!" Jesus had become front page news.

Realize, this isn't the first time Jesus had been to the temple. Jesus had been coming to the temple every year since His birth. When

He came into the temple this time, it was not that he observed something that He hadn't seen before, many times before. The selling of animals and the exchanging of money had been going on for decades. His own parents had to wait in long lines for the moneychangers and to pay the overinflated prices for temple animals throughout His upbringing. Jesus doesn't get riled up because something new or different is happening in the temple.

What is different is that this is the first time Jesus had entered the temple after His ministry had been launched with His baptism by John in the Jordan River. Jesus entered the temple for the first time as Messiah, the Son of God. I understand, He had always been that, even on those other occasions with His parents, but the Father had never "let Him loose" before this time to start His public ministry. So, in that sense, this visit is a first and very unique.

When we look at the parallel accounts, we discover that this is not the only time Jesus cleansed the temple. The other three gospels record the second cleansing of the temple in Matt. 21:12ff, Mark 11:15ff, and Luke 19:45ff. Only John records *this* event, and there is some debate about this. Some scholars believe John is just putting this event out of context for literary purposes, but I believe there is enough extraneous evidence to indicate two cleansings. For our purposes here, I'm not going to go into those arguments.

This cleansing took place at the outset of Jesus's ministry. The second cleansing took place at the conclusion of His ministry. These "bookend" events tell us much about God's attitude regarding public worship. When we corporately gather to worship our Holy Father, it should be with solemnity, humility, and a prayerful attitude regarding our dependence upon Him. There is no place for self-seeking or self-aggrandizement when we come to worship. Our focus must not be up-front but up above. The focus must be on what we can give Him, not what we can gain for ourselves. If you observe carefully, way too much "worship" that goes on today is more of a performance for the audience than it is an offering to God.

Tension Begins to Mount

As Jesus entered the temple and passed through Solomon's Porch into the Court of the Gentiles, He took notice of the myriad of booths for the selling of sacrificial animals set up all around Solomon's Porch. Long lines of pilgrims had formed, waiting to exchange their money and buy their sacrificial animals. The animals used for sacrifices had to be spotless, perfect animals. Of course, for those coming from afar, it was difficult, if not impossible, to bring their own animals. If anyone did bring his own animal, it must first be inspected by the priests to see if it "passed muster" as a flawless specimen. The chances were slim that it would.

The word *moneychanger* means money-banker or money-broker. Every Israelite or proselyte, rich or poor, who had reached the age of twenty was obligated to pay a half shekel into the sacred treasury as an offering to Jehovah. This tribute was in every case to be paid in the exact Hebrew half shekel. At Passover, everyone in the world who was an adult male and wished to worship at the temple would bring this offering and purchase a sacrificial animal at the temple. Since there was no acceptance of foreign money, because of the foreign images on them, the moneychangers would sell "temple coinage" at a very high rate of exchange and assess a fixed charge for their services. This amounted to a double charge. A charge for the exchange rate and a charge for the service of the exchange.

The judges who sat to inspect the offerings that were brought by the pilgrims were quick to detect any blemish in them they could find. This was expensive for the wealthy pilgrims and was ruinous for the poor who could only offer a turtledove or pigeon. There was no defense for them or court of appeal since the priestly authorities took a large percentage on every transaction.[85] There were plenty of moneychanger booths around to accommodate your needs for exchang-

---

[85] http://www.bible-history.com/gentile_court/TEMPLECOURTJesus_and_the_Temple.htm

ing currency. But beware, the exchange rate was extreme. This was probably the greatest source of income for the priestly class. And it was a rip-off for every Jew.

A Volcanic Eruption

As Jesus slowly walked along Solomon's Porch, observing the exchange of currency and the selling of animals at inflated prices, observing especially the expressions of distress and bewilderment on faces of the masses of poor who couldn't afford the rates, a sense of the injustice and the greed of it all began to build in Jesus's chest. He felt with clarity the indignation of His Father. This had nothing to do with honoring or worshipping His Father. It had only to do with lining the pockets of the temple priests at the expense of true worshippers and especially the poor and vulnerable. They were using His Father's house as a front to rob the common folks! This was horribly wrong on every front.

Quietly, without saying a word, Jesus began to pick up some stiff cords that had been used to tether animals and bind crates of birds. He silently, almost subconsciously, began to weave the cords into a whiplike scourge. He did this as He silently strolled along observing the commerce. His disciples noticed what He was doing but just assumed He was "doodling." His brow began to furrow deeply.

Then all of a sudden, Jesus erupted in anger. He suddenly began to holler at these moneychangers and vendors, accusing them of making His Father's house a house of merchandise. It was supposed to be a house of prayer. They had made it a den of thieves. As He accused them of robbing the people, He began to turn the tables over and lash out with his homemade whip. The stinging bite of the cords brought a painful awareness of His anger as the whip hit its targets. Welts began to immediately appear on the unsuspecting victims. Men screamed in agony as fear and confusion raced through the concessions.

Some had no idea who He was. Many recognized Him as the Rabbi that had begun to establish a reputation among the common folks in Jerusalem. As He continued to walk through Solomon's Porch, tables went crashing, money went flying, and the animals began to scatter in every direction. Cages containing the birds cracked open, setting them free. Oxen, bulls, and sheep began to flee along with the vendors.

His authority seemed unstoppable. As tables tipped over and money went clattering across the stone floor, the moneychangers began to panic. Some went scrambling for the loose coins while others were pushing and shoving, trying to avoid the sting of His scourge. He was relentless, chasing them completely from the temple. Along with the moneychangers and vendors, the animals scattered in every direction. All the while He kept repeating, *"Take these things away. Stop making My Father's house a place of business."*

It was clear to the multitude that was observing this event that His wrath was directed at those moneychangers and vendors who were involved in commerce. In verse 16, Jesus seemed to be particularly perturbed at those selling doves. In the other three accounts of the second cleansing, those selling doves are again called out. And for good reason. Doves were sold to the poorest of worshippers. These were the ones who were being ripped off the most. These were the ones being denied the opportunity to make the appropriate sacrifices and were condemned to live in their sin because they couldn't afford to pay the elevated fees. Not only was the exchange of money nowhere required in the law, but the elevated price of temple animals added insult to injury. Who were these priests who thought they were the ones who could prevent true worshippers from access to their God? Jesus's blood was boiling at this gross injustice imposed in His Father's name.

There was no rebuke of the people. In fact, He went out of His way to make sure that the "folks" were spared His wrath. But it was bedlam and chaos all mixed into one for those priests and temple officials.

Stunned Embarrassment

Jesus's disciples stood in stunned silence. What was He doing? This is insane. This was politically wrong! There had to be a better way to address this issue. Couldn't He have filed some kind of formal complaint and let this go through normal channels? The temple police will throw them all in jail. But where are the temple police? Don't they know what's going on here?

In all likelihood, this whole scene took place over the span of only several minutes. Given the extreme crowds and normal "chaos" of the Passover, the temple guards were already occupied and unavailable. Why someone didn't stand up to Jesus and push back was probably due to the fact that Jesus spoke with compelling authority.

In any event, as the disciples stood back and watched this melee go on, it hit them like a ton of bricks:

17. *His disciples remembered that it was written, "ZEAL FOR YOUR HOUSE WILL CONSUME ME."*

As His disciples quietly muttered among themselves, trying to figure out what was really going on, they remembered the passage from Psalm 69. They had memorized it as young boys in Awana. (You don't think they had Awana in Jesus's day?). It described one of the defining character traits of the Messiah that God would send. But they never thought that this was how it would manifest itself. It was as though Jesus could not help Himself when He saw the corruption and sin that was integral with the temple use. This was a deep offense to both Him and His Father.

Soon, Jesus's "rant" (for they did not know what else to call it) subsided as the moneychangers and merchants ran for cover in every direction, their animals scattering with them and coins bouncing everywhere across the Court of the Gentiles.

What "Sign" of Authority?

It wasn't long before the Jewish authorities showed up to confront Jesus:

> 18. *The Jews then said to Him, "What sign do You show us, seeing that you do these things?"*

I'm fascinated that they don't just tackle Him and hold Him down until the temple guards could arrive to put Him under arrest. But Jesus's popularity among the common folks had already begun to put some restraint on the response of the Jewish leadership. Jesus was already recognized by many as a Rabbi, and that in itself required some decorum. So they questioned by what authority He chased off the moneychangers and created such a disturbance in the temple. Who did He think He was? They demanded proof of such authority. Some sign that indicated He had the right to disrupt well-established procedure.

It's interesting that here they demand a sign as proof of his authority to disrupt the temple business. Obviously, the sign of turning water to wine at the wedding feast in Cana some months earlier hadn't made an impact among the Jewish leadership.[86] In a couple of years, they would become sick of all the signs Jesus was performing, wishing He would quit doing signs before all men became His converts.[87] During the remainder of the week of Passover, at this time, Jesus would do many more signs, demonstrating His authority.[88]

Jesus response to "what sign" is both profound and predictive:

> 19. *Jesus answered them, "Destroy this temple, and in three days I will raise it up."*

---

[86] John 2:1–12
[87] John 11:47–48
[88] John 2:23

20. *The Jews then said, "It took forty-six years to build this temple, and will You raise it up in three days?"*
21. *But He was speaking of the temple of His body.*
22. *So when He was raised from the dead, His disciples remembered that He said this; and they believed the Scripture and the word which Jesus had spoken.*

We all know from this side of the cross that Jesus was referring to His crucifixion and resurrection. It is obvious that from the very beginning Jesus knew exactly who He was and where He was going. He said this prophetically, and this statement would have its full intended impact in due time.

It is equally clear, from the Jews' response and the comment in verse 22, that Jesus's statement went right over the heads of both the Jewish leadership and His own disciples. You would think, in a spirit of communication and clarity, that Jesus should have said, "Crucify Me, and in three days, I will rise again!" That would have been clear, definitive, and to the point, would it not? The Jews' response might have been, "You're nuts. No one is going to crucify anyone. We don't even have the authority to crucify! What are you talking about?" It seems to me that a clearer response on Jesus's part would have made much more sense. Wouldn't you agree?

So why does Jesus make this obscure, seemingly ridiculous statement? For one obvious reason. God is looking for men and women who will study the Word of God to show themselves workmen, approved for every good service.[89] He is looking for followers who will think, and think deeply, about the truths of scripture. He's not interested in "believers" who live on the basis of clichés.

This response of the Jews reminds me of the young man that came into the pastor's office and said, "Pastor, would you please pray for my hearing?" "Of course," the Pastor replied. Then he placed each of his hands over both ears of the young man and began to

---

[89] 2 Timothy 2:15

pray. He implored God to heal the young man's hearing and to release him from this bondage. After a lengthy and impassioned prayer, the pastor released the young man, sat back, and said, "So, my son. How is your hearing?" The young man wrinkled his brow, thought for a brief moment, and replied, "I really don't know. It's not until next Friday."

That expresses the quick, thoughtless response of these Jewish leaders. Jesus's statement about rebuilding the temple in three days should have caused them to think just a bit instead of simply reacting.

An Honest Response

What would have been the honest response to Jesus's statement about destroying the temple and rebuilding it in three days? The thought process might have gone something like this. "Well, that's ridiculous. That is physically impossible. It took forty-six years to build this temple. Either Jesus thinks He is God, because only God could rebuild the temple in three days, or He is deluded, a nut job, or this must be some kind of metaphor or figure of speech with some other meaning." So why doesn't the Jewish leadership ask Him what He really means by this statement?

For whatever reason, they don't do that. They quickly jump to the wrong conclusion. They think Jesus is talking literally about the temple. In defense of the Jewish leadership, Jesus was here opening up a concept (that our bodies were intended to be temples of God's Spirit) that was nowhere mentioned or even eluded to in the Old Testament. The idea of the human body being a temple of the Holy Spirit is only a New Testament concept.[90] This is why they immediately jumped to a literal interpretation of Jesus's statement, but I would still insist that an honest seeker would have pursued the meaning of His comment rather than jumping to the literal interpretation as they did.

---

[90] 1 Corinthians 3:16, 6:19

John explains in verse 22 the impact this comment had on the disciples. Jesus is about two years away from the resurrection at this point, but here is an interesting insight about understanding the scriptures. You may read something in the scriptures today and not really understand what it means. That's OK. It may need to take two years to marinate in your thinking before the sense of it comes to light. Even a good steak takes time to marinate. That's one of the real values of studying scriptures over time. (They build upon themselves.) John says the result of this revelation, after Jesus's resurrection, was that the disciples were convinced of both the truth of the written scriptures (the Old Testament) and the words that Jesus spoke.

Many Believed What?

In verses 23–25, John gives us a brief insight into the remainder of the week of Passover for Jesus:

23. *Now when He was in Jerusalem at the Passover, during the feast, many believed in His name, observing His signs which He was doing.*
24. *But Jesus, on His part, was not entrusting Himself to them, for He knew all men,*
25. *and because He did not need anyone to testify concerning man, for He Himself knew what was in man.*

The reference to the signs Jesus was doing in Jerusalem is curious. We aren't told anything more than that He was "doing signs." Most likely the signs involved healings of one sort or another. We are told, however, as a result of those signs, many were believing. It is interesting how John uses the term *believing*. It doesn't necessarily mean they were becoming "Christians." In fact, we will discover in chapter 8 that many who "believed" had no place in their hearts for the Word of God, that they really despised Jesus and wanted to kill

Him, that their real allegiance was to their *"father the devil."*[91] That's not exactly a "believer" in the evangelical sense of the word!

What did they believe? Most likely, they believed what Nicodemus believed, revealed in the following chapter, that Jesus was a teacher sent from God because no one could do the signs that He was doing if God were not with Him.[92] That's a far cry from believing He was God's Messiah, God in the flesh, and placing their faith and trust in Him! God had sent many prophets in the past that could do signs. Yet they despised and killed them.[93]

Another kind of contrast is set up here in verses 23–25. On the one hand, many were believing in Jesus; but on the other hand, Jesus wasn't entrusting Himself to them. From the paragraph above, it is obvious why Jesus wasn't entrusting Himself to men. Jesus knew what was in the heart of man. This is not a supernatural "knowing" but a simple, wise understanding of the character of fallen human nature as revealed in the Old Testament. He knew men were fickle, sinful, selfish, and always put themselves first. This was clearly taught throughout the Old Testament. The heart of man was desperately wicked and deceitful above all things.[94] Jesus knew that their "belief" would not necessarily result in saving grace.

He knew the reason they "believed in his name" was because He was doing signs. They "believed" because of what they could get for themselves, not because they trusted Him. They just saw Him as their personal genie. Their belief was self-focused. That is exactly why much later many of His "disciples" would desert Him.[95]

Jesus will only entrust Himself to those who entrust themselves to Him. That is as true today as it was 2,100 years ago. If you want all that Jesus has to offer, you better be prepared to give to Jesus all that you have to offer, and I mean everything—your entire heart,

---

91 John 8:31, 37, 44
92 John 3:2
93 Nehemiah 9:26, Luke 11:47, Acts 7:52, 1 Thessalonians 2:15
94 Jeremiah 17:9
95 John 6:66

soul, mind, and strength.[96] The whole concept of salvation is based on an "exchanged life" principle. If you will give Him all of yourself, including all your sin, He will in exchange give you all of His righteousness.[97] But you must come to Him humbly, honestly, and with arms wide open.

The Bigger Picture

There is a very specific reason this scene follows directly after the water-to-wine miracle in John's gospel. From the larger point of view, the water-to-wine miracle shows us the very intention of the incarnation. God became flesh for the purpose of being sacrificed for our sin so that He might save us and take up residence within us. That is what is pictured by Jesus turning ordinary water into fine wine in ordinary stone pots.

But there is one prerequisite before the Lord can put the sweet wine of His Spirit into our stone-cold hearts. Those pots must first be emptied before they can be filled with God's Spirit. This was the whole point of John the Baptist's coming. He came to "prepare" the pots. The Baptizer came to cleanse those pots (through humble confession pictured by water baptism) so they could be filled by the One who came to baptize with the Spirit.[98] There can be no filling without first being cleansed of sin through heartfelt confession and repentance.

The cleansing of the temple is a symbolic picture of this very fact. John even tells us that Jesus was speaking of the temple of His body. Every man's body is a potential temple of God, but before God can fill us with His Spirit, we must first be cleansed. Sin must be confessed. Forgiveness must be sought. God desperately wants to fill your inner man with His Holy Spirit. Confession and repentance

---

[96] Mark 12:30
[97] 2 Corinthians 5:21
[98] John 1:33

is the only impediment preventing that reality. The temple of your heart must be cleansed before it can be filled. It is as simple as that.

Application

There are four important lessons that come out of this text. The first is that Jesus wasn't restricted in His response to wrongdoing because of political correctness. He didn't file a complaint with the Temple Registry Office of Abusive Tactics about the greed and corruption that was ripping the people off. He decided to take action personally and let the chips fall where they would. He saw injustice and decided to face it head-on.

Unfortunately, our culture has all but nullified the impact of our Christian influence today because of our fear of not being politically correct or of being labeled as a bigot, racist or having some kind of phobia. We would rather tolerate wrong than be labeled a racist. We would rather ignore the truth than be called a homophobe. We would rather allow the unborn innocent to die than be classified as part of the "war on women." The truth is no longer more important than our need to be accepted by our peers. We would rather let the poor suffer or let the injustice continue than speak out against it. Try being a "truth-teller" this week instead of a "people-pleaser."

Second, if you ever want Jesus to "entrust" Himself to you, then get your dirty heart clean, really clean. Come humbly before your Savior, confessing your sins, all of them. Realize that God can never fill you prior to you being cleansed. So, get cleansed!

Third, don't be so quick to "jump to conclusions" in your study of God's word. As you study your scriptures, the Spirit of God may speak things into your heart that may seem to be confusing. Avoid the temptation to jump to conclusions. Let the Word of God ruminate in your mind and heart. Practice the art of meditating on God's word *and* give it time. It may take two years, but in God's time, He will let you understand what He thinks is important for you to understand.

I am personally convinced that one of the reasons so many cults have evolved is because men are impatient and demand quick answers from God. The truth is, God is not compelled or obligated to give us any answers. He is not beholden to us. A really good Lutheran friend of mine, a man who served in a position of leadership in his church for years, converted to Mormonism because he couldn't get his mind wrapped around the doctrine of the Trinity. Really?! It blows me away that so many in Christendom think they need to know everything God knows. That's just insane. Let God work on your heart—for your "whole" life.

Finally, why do you go to church? This one may be a stretch, but a stretch worth making. Almost everyone I run into goes to church to *get* something out of it. They are looking for a good, stimulating sermon, a great music set before the sermon, or they want their kids to have a great time in Sunday school. Is any of this wrong? Maybe. Most churchgoers are there for the same reasons the moneychangers and vendors were at the temple: just to get something out of it. Don't misunderstand. We need and should be "blessed" when we gather as a church. But how about a motivation of giving, instead of getting, when we attend church next week?

It was that very attitude that angered our Lord so much. The "getting" mind-set turns our place of worship into something it was never intended to be. It turns our worship leaders into performers whose job it is to entertain us or preachers whose job it is to "tickle our ears." How about adopting the attitude, when gathering to worship, of *giving*? What I mean is, coming to church, first to give our prayers and offerings of thanksgiving to the Lord, allowing it to become again a house of prayer, then turning our attention to giving to those around us. Even giving to those we don't know or have just met. Wouldn't it be refreshing to seek out their needs and concerns of others instead of being so willing to readily express our needs and concerns?

Somehow, if we could adopt a *giving* instead of a *getting* attitude when it comes to corporate worship, our lives would change for the better regardless of the music set, the sermon, or whether our churches are growing numerically. When you go to church this week, purposefully seek to be an encouragement or blessing on one other person before you leave.

CHAPTER 8

When Great Minds Meet
John 3:1-15

There is probably nothing more venerated among men in our society today than wealth, power, and intellect. The names of the rich and famous are common household names. Who hasn't heard of Bill or Hillary Clinton, Donald Trump, Bill Gates, Paul Allen, or Mark Zuckerberg to name just a few? They all rub shoulders with those who mold and shape society, and most men envy their positions of influence and power. I just envy Paul Allen's boat!

Many have been led to believe that fame and fortune, and the power and influence that they bring, are the secrets of happiness and fulfillment. But scores of the rich and famous have proven that wrong. Robin Williams hanged himself in his home in San Francisco. Curt Cobain, the rock star from the group Nirvana, shot himself in the head. Jovan Belcher, Kansas City Chiefs linebacker, shot first his girlfriend and then himself in the head. And who will ever forget the fall of OJ Simpson, Whitney Houston, Tiger Woods, or Senator John Edwards?

This raises a very important issue. What is it, way deep down inside (I mean *way* deep down), that is the most important thing in your life? What is it at the very bottom that gives you a sense of purpose and meaning? Is it something transitory like position, power, money, or influence? Whatever makes you "tick" needs to be something solid and immoveable. Something that time and pressure can't distort. Even something eternal. That's what you need to anchor your life to.

That brings us to Nicodemus, one of the better-known Jews in the gospel records. In his day, Nicodemus would be among the class of the rich and famous listed above. He was a man of great influence, a member of the ruling class, very wealthy, and powerful, but there was much more that was buried deep in Nicodemus's soul.

As you read on, you will discover that Nicodemus was a lonely man, a man who longed for something he couldn't define, a very frustrated and confused man. He was a man searching for truth that seemed to elude his great intellect. "The meaning of life" had escaped his grasp. He had more creature comforts than most of us will ever have in all our lives, but there was a quiet desperation in his heart. It was an unsettling feeling that something was wrong; something was missing. I would suggest that there are multitudes of "wealthy, popular, powerful" people alive today that have both the comforts and the emptiness that haunted Nicodemus. I dare say, many of those I've listed above were or are in this category.

The story of Nicodemus opens abruptly in the first two verses of chapter three:

1. *Now there was a man of the Pharisees, named Nicodemus, a ruler of the Jews;*
2. *this man came to Him by night, and said to Him, "Rabbi, we know that You have come from God as a teacher; for no one can do these signs that You do unless God is with him."*

A Pharisee

Verse 1 gives us the first two clues about Nicodemus. First, we learn he was a Pharisee. If there ever existed a group that could be called religious fanatics, it would be the Pharisees of the Jews.

Becoming a Pharisee was a lifelong commitment. To become a Pharisee, you had to take a solemn vow before three eyewitnesses that you would devote every moment of your entire life to obeying the Ten Commandments. The Pharisees took this commitment very seriously. Strict obedience to the Ten Commandments was their idea of what was required to be pleasing to God. Like most who achieve great success in life, Nicodemus was a driven man.

If you think about the Ten Commandments for a moment, they are stated in rather simple terms: Thou shall not kill. Thou shall not commit adultery. Thou shall not covet, etc. In order to be more specific, so as not to violate any of the laws, it was felt that they needed to define those laws so they would know how to apply them to specific situations in life.

So there grew up in Israel a group of men called scribes. Scribes were a subset of the Pharisees. These men spent their entire lives studying the Ten Commandments. It was their mission to figure out how they should apply each commandment to situations in everyday life. That way, the Pharisees could be sure they were being obedient to the law.

Scribes took their job very seriously. In fact, they compiled a very thick book, which the Jews have to this day, called the Mishnah. The Mishnah is divided into sections according to each of the Ten Commandments. It was designed to help you know how to obey each commandment.

If you have ever seen or tried to read some of the United State Internal Revenue Service Tax Code, you would know what I am talking about. Or I'm sure you've seen on television the enormous volume of information that is the Affordable Care Act (Obama Care). It would take a rocket scientist to read through either and an Einstein to understand them.

In the Mishnah, the law about not working on the Sabbath (just one of the Ten Commandments) consists of twenty-four chapters. To help clarify things, in addition to the Mishnah, the scribes came up with the Talmud. The Talmud is a commentary on the Mishnah to help you understand it. In the Talmud, there are 156 pages on the definition of what keeping the Sabbath means. So you can see that the Pharisees were serious about keeping the law.

For example, the scribes decreed that any form of labor in which a man made his living on a daily basis was forbidden on the Sabbath. Therefore if a farmer tethered his animal during the week by tying a knot, he could not tie a knot on the Sabbath. The same was true for a sailor.

There were some exceptions, however. If tying a knot was absolutely necessary for life on the Sabbath, it was permitted. Also, if you could tie a knot with one hand, it was permitted on the Sabbath.

No one could make mortar on the Sabbath. That was considered to be work. If you spat in the dirt on the Sabbath, that was making mortar and a violation of the Sabbath law. You could spit on a rock, but only if there was no dirt on the rock. So you had to be a pretty good aim at spitting on the Sabbath.

These minute rules went on and on and had become very burdensome on the people, but this was how committed Nicodemus was in his quest to be pleasing to God. Obeying the law of God was the primary focus of his life. That's what gave Nicodemus meaning in life. It was what he lived for.

There is a second thing we learn about Nicodemus in verse 1. He was a "ruler of the Jews." This is a specific term meaning that Nicodemus was a member of the Great Sanhedrin. Not only was he uniquely one of the six thousand Pharisees that existed at that time (they limited themselves to that number), but he was also one of the seventy members of the Great Sanhedrin. The Sanhedrin was the supreme ruling body for Jews all over the world. They were the unique ruling class of all of Judaism.

A Night Visit

Verse 2 sets up the situation. Here we learn immediately at least three things about Nicodemus. First, he came to Jesus at night; second, he believed that Jesus was a teacher (that's what a rabbi is) who had come from God; and third, it was the miracles that Jesus had done that convinced Nicodemus that Jesus had come from God.

It is my belief that many misunderstand Nicodemus because of the fact that he came to Jesus by night. They quickly jump to the conclusion that Nicodemus was motivated by fear, or he was cowardly. Of course, Jesus had just trashed the temple, but more than anger, the reaction of the Jewish leadership was confusion.

Neither fear nor cowardice motivated Nicodemus to come to Jesus by night. He wasn't fearful of anything or anyone. In John 7, when the hatred of Jesus had risen to the boiling point and the discussion in the Sanhedrin arose about killing Jesus, it was Nicodemus who stood before his peers and defended Him.[99] After the crucifixion of Jesus, Nicodemus was one of the two that went before Pilate to ask for the body of Jesus.[100] A man doesn't rise to the stature of Nicodemus by avoiding confrontation and living by fear or by being a coward. So why by night?

The reason Nicodemus came to Jesus by night is really quite simple, with far less drama. Nicodemus worked a sixteen to eighteen hour day. He was constantly in demand. He was a "rock star" in his day, and wherever he went, people gathered. He was constantly barraged by questions and people seeking his counsel. He had services to attend, meetings to go to, ceremonies to oversee, discussions with officials to attend. On and on Nicodemus's day went. No one's calendar was more crammed than his.

Yet Jesus was equally busy. Throngs of people constantly crowded around Him. Everyone was seeking to be healed, cured, helped, or blessed. His own disciples were always there, asking questions. He was teaching and preaching at every opportunity. People were constantly asking questions, wanting Him to talk to them and explain things. His calendar was every bit as busy as Nicodemus's.

---

[99] John 7:48–52
[100] John 19:38–39

It was practically impossible for Nicodemus to meet up with Jesus during the daylight hours without thousands of folk crushing in to find out what was being said. Everyone wanted to listen in. These were two of the most popular men on the planet. It would be like Paul Murray and Jerry Laursen wanting to have a private conversation in the foyer after church service (I'm kidding, of course!).

The only way Nicodemus could get some quality one-on-one time with Jesus was to come at night when everyone else had gone to bed. In fact, it was the practice of Pharisees to do their studying at night when they could find some privacy. Night was the only practical time to come to Jesus and expect that privacy.

Nicodemus's attitude about Jesus, prior to his coming to Him, is clearly stated in verse 2. He believed that Jesus was a teacher who was sent from God. What convinced him were the signs that Jesus was able to do. They were clearly supernatural. It was not trickery or deception. No one could do the things Jesus was doing unless God was with Him. Even though the rumor was already beginning to spread among the Sanhedrin that the power was demonic and not divine, Nicodemus wasn't buying that. Nicodemus knew that demonic power enslaved, blinded, and twisted people's minds. The things Jesus was doing were redemptive, healing, and positive. That wasn't characteristic of demonic power. It had to be divine power.

Deep-Down Motivation

In verse 3, Jesus tells Nicodemus what the requirements were for entering the kingdom of God:

3. *Jesus answered and said to him, "Truly, truly, I say to you, unless one is born again, he cannot see the kingdom of God."*

The text reads as if Jesus just blurts this out without any context. I don't believe that is true. I believe there is a great deal of context that leads Jesus to respond to Nicodemus with this statement. The very fact that the text says, *"Jesus answered,"* implies that conversation had been going on before this answer. All of this begs the question as to what really drove Nicodemus to come to Jesus in the first place. That motivation is revealed here in verse 3.

This isn't rocket science. Nicodemus was one of the most brilliant biblical minds alive at his time. He was fully aware of the signs Jesus was doing. He was also fully aware of John the Baptist's amazing and widespread ministry. He understood that John's message of baptism was a preparatory act for the coming of the Messiah (at least that was the Baptizer's opinion). Nicodemus understood the Old Testament scriptures that spoke of a ministry like the Baptizer's preceding the coming of the Messiah.[101] He was fully aware of the vision John's father, Zachariah, had in the temple prior to John's birth. The Sanhedrin to that day was probably still debating what really happened to Zachariah.

Nicodemus was also fully aware of the magi that had come from the east to worship a "newborn king of the Jews."[102] He was every bit as familiar with the scriptures that brought those magi from the east to Israel as the magi were. He had heard about the shepherds coming to the manger and the angelic choir the shepherds claimed to have heard. He knew of the "slaughter of the innocents" ordered by Herod the Great. Nicodemus was not an idiot.

On Nicodemus's desk at home was a scroll of Daniel opened to Daniel 9:24–26:

24. *Seventy weeks have been decreed for your people and your holy city, to finish the transgression, to make an end of sin, to make atonement for iniquity, to bring in everlasting righteousness, to seal up vision and prophecy and to anoint the most holy place.*
25. *So you are to know and discern that from the issuing of a decree to restore and rebuild Jerusalem until Messiah the Prince there*

---

[101] Malachi 3:1, Isaiah 40:3
[102] Matthew 2:1–2

will be seven weeks and sixty-two weeks; it will be built again, with plaza and moat, even in times of distress.

26. *Then after the sixty-two weeks the Messiah will be cut off and have nothing, and the people of the prince who is to come will destroy the city and the sanctuary. And its end will come with a flood; even to the end there will be war; desolations are determined.*

Nicodemus clearly understood that the time for the Messiah to come was *now*. If God's word was true and reliable, and Nicodemus believed it was, then somewhere in Israel the Messiah had to be present.

As far as Nicodemus was concerned, there were only two possibilities. The first was John the Baptist. That's why the contingent was sent from the Pharisees to question him, but John had flatly denied being the Messiah. The only other possibility was Jesus. Nicodemus had to get alone with Jesus to find out if He was really the Messiah.

Above all else, it was the talk of the nation, just as the terrorist bombing in France this week was on every TV channel and every radio news station, it was talked about in every coffee shop and bagel store in Jerusalem. (They didn't have TV back then? Really?) Everyone was talking about the kingdom of God. It was the main topic of conversation in the Great Sanhedrin. It was on everyone's mind.

Unlike the masses, Nicodemus's interest in Jesus wasn't for personal gain. He was genuinely interested in talking to Jesus about the kingdom of God. He needed to know, is this the time? Is Jesus the Messiah? Is the kingdom of God really at hand? The most important thing in Nicodemus's life was that he was a member in good standing in the kingdom of God. That's what drove him.

The "*we* know" in verse 2 is very revealing. It is the "we" of a group of Pharisees in the Sanhedrin. After the cleansing of the temple, there was probably some real soul-searching discussions in the Sanhedrin about what was really going on in the temple. The "we" had to be some contingent of the Sanhedrin with which Nicodemus identified. Nicodemus was not alone in believing that the signs Jesus had been doing were from God, and if they were from God, what might that imply about the coming kingdom of God?

The Kingdom Requirement

By the time we get to verse 3 in the text, it would seem that Nicodemus and Jesus had been talking for quite some time. Nicodemus had been questioning Jesus about the coming kingdom of God. In verse 3, Jesus decided to drive the point home about how one enters the kingdom of God. As He came to this extremely important point, He underscored the importance of His next statement by a common phrase, "Truly, truly, I say to you..."

What Jesus is saying to Nicodemus is "Listen up. Pay close attention. This is really important. If you miss this, you miss the whole meaning of the kingdom of God and how a man enters it." And it is at this point in the conversation that Jesus's eyes are locked squarely on the eyes of Nicodemus, assuring that He had Nicodemus's full attention. Both men sit relaxed in the dim candlelight, but the mood has grown more intense.

Jesus tells Nicodemus that the fundamental requirement for entering the kingdom of Heaven is that he must be "born again." This is a term that many believers have adopted today. We call ourselves "born-again believers." It is also a term that others have used to ridicule Christians, as though they are some kind of nutcases. Unbelievers ignorantly use this term for derision for the same reason Nicodemus does. They simply don't understand what Jesus was saying. Ridicule is often a cover for ignorance when you don't know what you are talking about.

Nicodemus's mind raced as he tried to understand what Jesus was saying. His first thought was, "Are you kidding me? Be born again? That's impossible? No, it's nonsensical. It's not just nonsensical, I believe it is ridiculous. What are You saying?" Nicodemus leaned forward in his chair just a bit. He was thrown by the emphasis Jesus put on this simple statement and how unrealistic it sounded. He struggled to find words to reply. He was baffled.

The words Jesus used for *born again* are interesting. The phrase can have three meanings for a Jew. It can mean "to do it again a second time." In other words, a repeat of the first process, being physically born again. This is the common understanding of this statement today. But the term can also mean "to begin radically, completely, all over, brand new; to have a new beginning." Nicodemus was an older man. To start all over again was impossible. There wasn't enough life left for him. That couldn't be what Jesus was asking. A third common meaning of the term was to be "born from above."

The meaning "born from above" occurs a couple other times in the New Testament. Peter used this term in speaking of newborn babes in Christ.[103] This was not a definition of *born again* that Nicodemus was unfamiliar with.

In fact, the concept of *born again* was a familiar term used in the mystery religions of Nicodemus's day. Even in Judaism, the idea of "rebirth" or being born again was a major tenant. When Gentiles were converted and baptized into Judaism, they were considered to be born again. Nicodemus was completely familiar with this concept. But he, being a Jew, didn't need to be born from above. He was a Jew, for goodness' sake. Only sinners, Gentiles, needed to be born from above. Jesus certainly couldn't mean that in Nicodemus's case.

What Jesus was asking seemed nonsensical to Nicodemus by any of the three meanings of the term. Was Jesus really asking Nicodemus to be born again; to make a whole, new, radical start; to be born from above; to be born of God?

Clearly, Jesus couldn't be referring to Nicodemus. Jesus seems to be talking to him as if he was a Gentile. Certainly, Jesus knew that he, Nicodemus, was a Pharisee. He had devoted his entire life to pleasing

---

[103] 1 Peter 1:23, 2:2

God. He had given everything to obey the law. Jesus could not have found a better Jew than Nicodemus.

Besides, Nicodemus was already one of God's chosen people, chosen from above. The Jews *were already* God's children. Their future inheritance was the kingdom of God. God had given His law to them, not to anyone else. Israel was a special and unique people.

Jesus Doesn't Understand

Jesus must not understand that Nicodemus had done everything known to man to demonstrate his worthiness to God. He was not only "the teacher"[104] of Israel, but a privileged member of the esteemed Great Sanhedrin. If you think becoming president of the United States is difficult, try becoming a member of the Sanhedrin.

He had studied the law of God endlessly. He had kept every letter of the law that he could. He gave generously to the temple. He made commitment after commitment to serve others. He taught all he knew. He served the people continuously. He had done everything humanly and physically possible to be part of the kingdom of God and to please God.

To suggest that Nicodemus had to start over was ludicrous to him. In fact, it was downright insulting. No one had ever talked to Nicodemus like that! Oh yes. He was familiar with the term. But for Jesus to suggest that He was talking about Nicodemus went straight to his pride. Jesus couldn't be talking about him! Nicodemus's countenance began to sag as he slightly slumped in his chair and his brow began to furrow with resentment. Jesus just didn't understand him.

A side note here. One of the most difficult things for a nonbeliever to swallow when considering becoming a Christian is the truth that all their life, everything good they have ever done, all the kindness, generosity, and volunteerism they have done, counts for *nothing* from God's point of view. So many people think that God is going

---

[104] John 3:10

to weigh their good works against their bad works in the end. HE IS NOT! You *cannot* score "points" with God under any circumstance. Citizenship in the kingdom of God is a gift. There is nothing anyone can ever do to earn it. This is where Jesus is going in this discussion, and Nicodemus is sensing it. Not only do your "good deeds" count for nothing, they are considered by God as "filthy rags!"[105] That's the pill Nicodemus is having a hard time swallowing, and that is why Nicodemus's follow-up reply is somewhat sarcastic:

4. *Nicodemus said to him, "How can a man be born when he is old? He cannot enter a second time into his mother's womb and be born, can he?"*

What a strange reply. This passage is generally interpreted as Nicodemus thinking that Jesus was telling him that he must be born again physically. But wait a minute! Do you really think that is what Nicodemus thinks? The very concept is ludicrous at face value. No, Nicodemus is pushing back here.

Nicodemus is not ignorant of the other valid meanings of the term *born again*. He makes this comment in verse 4 "tongue-in-cheek." His pride had taken a pretty serious hit by Jesus. He's offended that Jesus had just told him that all his life's work was useless and that it counted for nothing in entering the kingdom of God. Since Jesus had just dismissed the entire meaning of Nicodemus's life, Nicodemus pushes back at Jesus by defining the term as physical rebirth.

Two Births

In verse 5, Jesus doesn't take the counter lightly. Now it is Jesus shifting in his chair, leaning a bit forward, fixed on Nicodemus. He double-downs on His comment and firmly tells Nicodemus unless

---

[105] Isaiah 64:6

that condition is met no one, even Nicodemus, will ever enter God's kingdom:

20. *Jesus answered, "Truly, truly, I say to you, unless one is born of water and the Spirit, he cannot enter into the kingdom of God."*

Jesus begins His response by repeating the same phrase twice. This is designed to grab Nicodemus by the intellectual collar and bring him up short: "Truly, truly, I say to you." Jesus is telling Nicodemus in no uncertain terms, "Don't trivialize this, Nicodemus. I'm serious! I hope I have your attention because I'm not talking about general theology, I'm speaking to you. What I am saying is true about you and applies to YOU!"

Then Jesus goes on to explain in verse 5 what he means by "born again." There are two parts to it. Birth number one is to be "born of water." Birth number two is to be "born of the Spirit." So the question comes up, "What does Jesus mean by 'born of water'?"

Many think Jesus means being born physically. They believe He is referring to the breaking of the water sack that protects the baby prior to birth, but that is not what Jesus is saying or referring to. He is not talking about human physical birth. Verse 6 is not a parallel of verse 5. When Jesus says "born of water," the first thing that jumps into Nicodemus's mind is *not* physical birth.

"Didn't you hear what Nicodemus just said in verse 4?" you will say. "He was talking about physical birth," and I will agree with you. But Nicodemus says that out of frustration and resistance to Jesus's argument. He is much smarter than that. Think about it for a minute. Physical birth is a requirement for getting into the kingdom of God. What does that mean? Were we "spirit beings," as the Mormons believe, before we were born physically and needed to first be put into a body by physical birth as a condition of entering the kingdom of God? That is ridiculous right out of the gate! To say I must be born physically before I can be born spiritually is like saying I must be alive before I can die! That is a nonsensical argument. In fact, it's no argument at all.

When Jesus refers to being "born of water," he is talking about the cleansing baptism of John the Baptist. This had been the talk of Jerusalem, Judea, and all of Samaria for weeks. The vast multitudes that had gone out to be baptized by John had been the talk of the entire area. It was on everyone's mind. It reminded Nicodemus of what was required of a Gentile to become part of the people of God. Gentiles were required to be cleansed before they could become Jews. They were "born again." John's baptism was a baptism of repentance. It was symbolic of a spiritual cleansing. John himself had been preaching that his message of repentance of sin (symbolized in water baptism) was a necessary precursor of being baptized by the Spirit.

Jesus is saying that the first thing necessary in being born from above is the need to repent and confess our sins. It is as simple as that. We must first come before God and humbly confess (agree with God) that there is nothing in us that we can offer that is pleasing to Him. We must recognize that all have sinned and fallen short of the glory of God, that "there is none righteous, no not one." Not even Nicodemus!

That was the conclusion the Apostle Paul came to in 2 Corinthians 3. He realized that he was not adequate in himself to consider anything as coming from himself. He couldn't earn his way into God's kingdom. No human effort, dedication, study, education, accomplishment, position, status, wealth, or understanding qualifies anyone, even Nicodemus, for God's kingdom.

The place to start for Nicodemus, or any Jew or Gentile if they desire to enter God's kingdom, is to repent and confess their sins. That is what paves the way, makes the path straight, for us to be filled with His Spirit. That's what Jesus meant, that we must be first "born of water." We must come to God with a humble, repentant heart. That is what John's baptism represented.

After confession comes birth number two. We must be born of the Spirit of God. Born from above means born from "heaven/

God." God can and will do what man cannot do for himself. A man can't be born of the spirit on his own. That is impossible, and being born of the Spirit obviously results in spiritual life. If you have never been born from above, you are by definition, spiritually dead!

Jesus reads in Nicodemus's expression and body language that he is surprised that a spiritual birth is necessary for access to the kingdom of God. So Jesus explains a little further about this requirement for entering the kingdom of God:

6. *That which is born of flesh is flesh, and that which is born of the Spirit is spirit*

Most commentators and folks read this and think that what Jesus is saying is that which is born physically is physical and that which is born spiritually is spiritual. But is that what Jesus is really saying? I know that I have gone way out on a limb here with my approach to this passage, but let me go out just a bit further. Maybe it will give you something to think about.

I do not think Jesus is talking about physical birth and spiritual birth. The subject at hand is the kingdom of God. The subject is about the spiritual truth of what is fundamentally involved in becoming part of the kingdom of God.

When Jesus says, *"That which is born of the flesh,"* He is not referring to physical birth. He is referring to exactly what He says—our flesh, our sinful nature as men and that which the flesh produces. He is talking about the effect of that which comes from human reason, human effort, and human motivation. Jesus is still hammering away at the "work ethic" that Nicodemus thought qualified him for the kingdom of God. All that self-effort Jesus says, is only fleshly. It is useless. It is sinful. The flesh (human effort) can only produce "fleshly" (sinful) results. It cannot produce spiritual results. That which is born of (comes from) the flesh will always be fleshly. This is what Jesus is saying.

Nicodemus thought all his human effort and achievement (and because he was a Jew) had earned him a place in God's kingdom. He deserved a place in the kingdom of God simply because he was a Jew. This is exactly what Jesus is refuting here. Jesus is saying "No! You can't earn a place in God's kingdom. The flesh can only produce fleshly results. All of your righteousness is as filthy rags." That is what Jesus is telling Nicodemus.

On the other hand, that which is "of the spirit of God" (that which the Holy Spirit of God produces) will always produce *Godly* results. You must be born of the Spirit in order to produce spiritual results that are pleasing to God. It is only by this that any man enters the kingdom of God. "And, Nicodemus, you don't have God's Spirit in you. So you must be born again, by the Spirit of God, in order to enter His kingdom."

Perplexity

Small droplets of sweat had already begun to appear on Nicodemus's brow. His facial features had begun to tighten just a bit. His mind was racing. He was approaching information overload. Jesus saw the perplexity begin to form on Nicodemus's face. He had a look of bewilderment, confusion, and wonder all wrapped up in that wrinkled brow. So Jesus responded in an attempt to settle him just a bit:

7. *Do not marvel that I said to you, "You must be born again."*

Somehow, in all Nicodemus's vast learning he had failed to see this fundamental principle in the Old Testament. Yet books like the book of Joshua scream this reality. It was abundantly clear throughout the conquest of Canaan. Every victory was the result of what God had done. The whole conquest was a record of God working through His people to achieve His will. The only victory they tried to win in their own effort, in the flesh, was at Ai, and that was a complete and total disaster.

In the book of Job, Job learned that things, material and earthly possessions, meant nothing to God. It was only what God gave that had any significance. Throughout the Old Testament, only what God did through men had any value. Things that man did for God in an attempt to earn His pleasure meant nothing to Him. God wasn't interested in your whole burnt offerings. He was interested in a broken and contrite heart that He will not despise.[106] David learned that lesson. If God wasn't accomplishing His work through you, then the work you were doing for Him had no value. This was becoming painfully obvious to Nicodemus.

He should have seen all this. Why hadn't he seen these clear truths? Nevertheless, he had not! He was amazed at what Jesus was now telling him. It rang true in his mind, and he marveled that he hadn't seen it before. Jesus's statement, *"Do not marvel,"* was a tender yet stern rebuke. He was saying, "You should have known this as the leading teacher in Israel."

Jesus continues to explain further how the Spirit of God works:

8. *The wind blows where it wishes and you hear the sound of it, but do not know where it comes from and where it is going; so is everyone who is born of the Spirit.*

Jesus likens the ministry of the Spirit as being the wind. You can't see the wind physically just as you can't see the Spirit physically. You have no control over where the wind blows just as you have no control over what the Spirit may or may not do. You can see the effects of the wind, and you can also see the effects of the Spirit in a man's life. Those who are born of the Spirit can be identified by how the Spirit manifested Himself in their lives. Jesus will camp on this concept with His disciples when we get to John 15.

---

[106] Psalm 51:17

The Bottom Line

All of Nicodemus's life, he had done everything humanly possible to earn the favor of God. But it is only what the Spirit of God does that matters. And it is only the Spirit of God that can usher any man into the kingdom of God.

Nicodemus was stunned that he had never considered this before. He was completely perplexed by these simple truths:

9. *Nicodemus answered and said to Him, "How can these things be?"*

Clearly, everything Jesus was telling him about entering the kingdom of God, about being born again, and about what God will do for us as opposed to what we do ourselves, cut across the grain of everything Nicodemus had ever thought or believed. Nicodemus thought the kingdom of God would be a physical kingdom, not a spiritual kingdom. Nicodemus thought that the kingdom of God would only be for Jews.

Yet Jesus was talking as though *anyone* could be born again. That would mean that *anyone* could enter the kingdom of God. Nicodemus had always believed only Jews or those who proselytized into Judaism could enter the kingdom of God. Nicodemus thought observing the law was the only way to enter the kingdom of God. All that he thought that was sacred to him and available only to the Jews seemed to be melting away before his very eyes. He marveled at all this unnerving news. Even the candle next to him on the small table seemed to sag in unison with his posture.

Jesus responded to Nicodemus's question in a somewhat rebuking manner. There was no place for the self-pity that began to form in Nicodemus's mind:

10. *Jesus answered and said to him, "Are you the teacher of Israel, and do not understand these things?"*

Jesus was genuinely surprised at Nicodemus's lack of depth in this very important spiritual matter. Jesus implied that Nicodemus *should* have known all this. It had been foreshadowed in the Old Testament. As one of the leading teachers of Israel, Nicodemus had an obligation to show himself approved as a workman who could accurately handle the Word of Truth.[107]

Nicodemus was not just one of the six thousand Pharisees, but one of seventy members of the Great Sanhedrin. In addition, he was considered "the teacher" of Israel. He was the "go to" person when it came to understanding the Old Testament scriptures. He was a predominant member of an elite society, and he was wealthy, influential, and powerful. He was most likely one of those who sent the contingent of Jews to question John the Baptist. This information Jesus was sharing with Nicodemus was *not* beneath his pay grade.

So Jesus explained to Nicodemus why he had missed this:

11. *Truly, truly, I say to you, we speak that which we know, and bear witness of that which we have seen; and you do not receive our witness.*

For the third time, Jesus drills down on Nicodemus, telling him to listen carefully. This is the third "Truly, truly, I say to you." You have to be somewhat thick-headed to deserve this. Jesus is taking Nicodemus to school! This should *not* have been an "aha" moment for him. Isn't it interesting how you can read your Bible and miss so much? Yet that's exactly what Nicodemus had done. For me, this begs the question, *why?* How did this brilliant Bible scholar miss so much? What was Nicodemus's fundamental problem?

I don't think Nicodemus missed this because of a lack of intellect. Nicodemus missed it because he came to the scriptures with preconceived notions. He was a spiritual ideologue. His training had preconditioned him to read into the scriptures what *he* wanted them

---

[107] 2 Timothy 2:15

to say. He missed the actual truth because he didn't approach the scriptures with the attitude of "Here I am, Lord. Let me hear what you have to say." Like far too many Christians today, Nicodemus approached the scriptures with an agenda.

I was raised in a church that believed that you weren't saved if you hadn't been baptized by immersion. In fact, it was the very act of baptism that saved you. It was the doctrine of baptismal regeneration.

As a young believer, when I read the scriptures, I looked for and read into the scriptures' interpretations that supported that idea. I ignored and dismissed any passages that might suggest otherwise. When Ray Stedman and Dave Roper at Peninsula Bible Church, men I loved and admired, began to challenge my presupposition, it was very hard for me to accept what the Bible really said. It took me a long time to start reading the Bible with a genuine open mind and heart. It took a good two or three years to climb out of my religious traditions and accept the Bible for what it said without feeling guilty and without feeling as if I was abandoning my faith.

To be brutally honest, this is one of the dangers of a seminary or Bible college education. Clearly the PhDs that teach in these institutions are far more intelligent than the students that sit in their classes. But is the product of their instruction "indoctrination" or "teaching"? That may be a "sacred cow" we're not supposed to talk about, but Nicodemus was a product of "indoctrination," and he was indoctrinated at the best seminaries of his day.

What complicated things even more for Nicodemus was the fact that the traditions of the Jews had become as important (or more important) than what the scriptures actually taught.

This is what made Martin Luther's "revolt" so significant. It finally dawned on him that what the Catholic church was teaching didn't square with what the Bible taught. When Martin Luther decided to let the Bible speak to him directly, instead of the "teachings of the church," he was motivated to act, and his life radically changed. Was Martin Luther a brilliant biblical thinker before he grasped the truths in the book of Romans? Sure, he was. But like Nicodemus and being born again, Luther was ignorant about God's grace before he began to let the Bible speak for itself.

Jesus further confounds Nicodemus with the use of His pronouns. By using *we*, Jesus was referring to the testimony of the Father, Son, and Spirit. Nicodemus didn't miss that subtle innuendo. He had already accepted that Jesus had come from the Father. So Jesus bears down on that point. The import of this statement is stunning. Jesus is telling Nicodemus that *we*, the Father, Son, and the Holy Spirit, know what *we* are talking about and *we* are all in agreement. Secondly, *we* speak of what *we* have seen. *We* know this experientially. *We* have seen these truths played out in life.

Moral, Not Intellectual

The problem with Nicodemus was not that he didn't hear what Jesus was saying. It was as clear as the nose on his face, but he didn't want to accept it. It was not that he couldn't accept it, it was that he *wouldn't* accept it. It was an issue of his will, not his intellect.

I learned a very important lesson fifty years ago on the campus of San Jose State College when I was involved with Campus Crusade for Christ. We shared the gospel with literally hundreds and hundreds of students each semester using the *Four Spiritual Laws*. It became obvious to me that students didn't reject the gospel on intellectual grounds; they rejected the gospel on moral grounds. They didn't reject Jesus because they didn't understand what we were sharing. They rejected Jesus because they didn't want to admit they were sinners, and they didn't want their lifestyle to change. The gospel is always a moral issue, not an intellectual issue.

And that was Nicodemus's problem. He was having a real problem with accepting what Jesus was saying, not because he didn't understand it but because if *he did* understand it, it meant he would have to change. It meant he would have to be born again. It meant that everything he had previously believed would have to be changed, and how would that look for the leading Jew of Israel! It was a moral issue, not an intellectual issue.

Jesus continued to explain why Nicodemus had missed the point. What were the "earthly things" Jesus had just told Nicodemus about that he was having trouble believing? I believe, in the broader scope of this conversation of which we only have a snippet here, Jesus had talked about John's baptism and Nicodemus's need to embrace John's baptism of water as an act of repentance. The reason was because repentance was the requirement of being baptized by the Spirit. And only through this process will anyone see the kingdom of God.

If Nicodemus wouldn't believe these simple truths, how would he ever believe spiritual truth? That's what Jesus is saying. He can't talk to Nicodemus about the kingdom of God if he refuses to believe simple earthly truth.

Jesus's Real Authority

In verse 13, Jesus explained to Nicodemus the basis of the authority by which He spoke:

13. *And no one has ascended into heaven, but He who descended from heaven, even the Son of Man.*

This may sound confusing to you, but I think it made perfect sense to Nicodemus. *Son of Man* was a familiar term to Nicodemus. John uses the term twelve times in this gospel. Nicodemus knows that Jesus is talking about Messiah, the One God would send to earth. Most commentators think this is a reference to the incarnation of Jesus, but because the concept of ascension is primary in the statement, I believe what Jesus is referring to is ascension, not incarnation. It is the ascension of Jesus, not the incarnation of Jesus, that will prove beyond all doubt all Jesus taught. Of course, ascension assumes resurrection, which is the ultimate proof of all that Jesus said and did.

If His incarnation was true, but death defeated Him, then He would not have been Messiah. It's His ascension that makes it all make sense. The thing that will ultimately convince Nicodemus (and many others) that Jesus was indeed the Son of God who became flesh and dwelt among us will be His resurrection and ascension, not His incarnation. He really was Messiah. He really did come to seek and save the lost. The resurrection of Christ and His ascension back to heaven would put all doubt about His Messiahship to rest in the minds of genuine truth-seeking men. Men like Nicodemus.

Jesus illustrates for Nicodemus this truth from the Old Testament:

14. *And as Moses lifted up the serpent in the wilderness, even so must the Son of Man be lifted up;*
15. *that whoever believes may in Him have eternal life.*

This is clearly a reference out of an event that is recorded in Numbers 21. It would be helpful to look at that Numbers 21 passage beginning at verse 4:

4. *Then they set out from Mount Hor by the way of the Red Sea, to go around the land of Edom; and the people became impatient because of the journey.*
5. *The people spoke against God and Moses, "Why have you brought us up out of Egypt to die in the wilderness? For there is no food and no water, and we loathe this miserable food."*
6. *The LORD sent fiery serpents among the people and they bit the people, so that many people of Israel died.*
7. *So the people came to Moses and said, "We have sinned, because we have spoken against the LORD and you; intercede with the LORD, that He may remove the serpents from us." And Moses interceded for the people.*
8. *Then the LORD said to Moses, "Make a fiery serpent, and set it on a standard; and it shall come about, that everyone who is bitten, when he looks at it, he will live."*

9. *And Moses made a bronze serpent and set it on the standard;
and it came about, that if a serpent bit any man, when he
looked to the bronze serpent, he lived.*

How Moses (and God) put up with those ungrateful idiots in
the Old Testament is beyond me. I'm just thankful He puts up with
this often-ungrateful idiot! It was the people's unwillingness to trust
God to enter the promised land at Kadesh Barnea that resulted in
this wandering in the first place. It was never God's will or desire for
His people to wander through the wilderness for forty years. But they
refused to obey and trust Him. So, here they are!

We learn in verses 4 and 5 that the people became impatient with
this wandering and began to grumble against God and Moses. They
began to "loathe this miserable food" (referring to the manna God
had graciously and supernaturally given them). They were ungrateful
for all that God had provided, even though they didn't deserve any
of it. So the Lord judged their rotten, ungrateful, self-centered attitudes. He sent fiery serpents among them as a judgment for their sin.

The serpent is always a symbol of sin in the Old Testament.
Jesus was referring to this event in the Old Testament where God
brought judgment upon Israel for their sin and that judgment came
in the form of serpents that infested the camp of Israel. Their bite
was lethal.

The people realized that they had sinned against God and
Moses, and they went to Moses in repentance, admitting their sin.
God instructed Moses to make a bronze serpent and put it atop a
large staff. As Moses lifted up that serpent on the staff, if the people looked upon the serpent, they would be saved from a certain
death. This was a picture of the sin of man being lifted up on a
wooden "staff."

Jesus used this as a symbolic example of the mission of the Son
of Man. The whole reason God became flesh and dwelt among us
was to be lifted up on a wooden "staff." That when He was lifted
up, He would take the sin of men upon Himself. Jesus was telling

Nicodemus that He is the fulfillment of this beautiful illustration (an actual event) that happened in the Old Testament.

Once Jesus was lifted up at His crucifixion, all who look upon His substitutionary death on the cross, accepting that death, by faith, as payment in full for their own personal sin, will also be saved from a certain and eternal death. That meant anyone, Jew or Gentile, slave or free, male or female. All who look upon Him with believing faith will be saved. They will be born again from above. And only those will see the kingdom of God. That's how you enter the kingdom of God. That's what it means to be born again.

Application

Entering the kingdom of God is really quite simple, but it is the most difficult thing you will ever do. There are only two requirements: two births. First, you must come to the realization that you are a sinner and desperately lost. Coming to that realization will be evidenced by your complete and humble confession and repentance by asking Jesus to forgive you of your own personal sin. Second, you must accept His substitutionary death on the cross, by faith, as payment in full for your sin. You must relinquish the control of your life to Him, submitting to Him as your Savior and Lord. That's how you enter the kingdom of God: repent and believe. At that point you will be born again from above. That is the second birth. It is really quite straightforward. Have you done that? If not, just do it!

CHAPTER 9

A Heavy Choice
John 3:16-21

There is probably no more famous verse in the Bible than John 3:16. You can hardly watch a Sunday afternoon football game without someone in the end zone holding up a sign that has John 3:16 written on it. Have you ever wondered why they were doing that and what they were trying to say? Me too!

In the text before us, Jesus continues His discussion with the leading teacher of the Jews, the Pharisee named Nicodemus, who was a member of the Great Sanhedrin. Jesus had just explained to Nicodemus that he must be born again. Not a physical rebirth, but he must be born again spiritually, and that spiritual rebirth first required a heartfelt repentance of sin.

This was a huge thing Jesus was asking of Nicodemus. He had spent his entire life believing that all the good works he had done, all the people he had taught, all the study he had accomplished, and his life commitment to obeying the Ten Commandments as a Pharisee had scored him high points in earning his way into the kingdom of God. But Jesus had said "NO!" None of that counted. None of that was worth anything or gained Nicodemus any credit in getting into the kingdom of God. You can't earn your way into God's kingdom. Good works earn you nothing with God.

Nicodemus was crestfallen and confused. He could hardly believe what Jesus was telling Him. His life commitment and work counted for nothing. "That can't be true!" he thought. To add insult to injury, Jesus was telling him he had to consider all of his efforts as sin and repent of them. wow!

But the condition of repentance (as John had preached in the wilderness) was absolutely essential. It was the one necessary step to placing faith in Jesus Christ as the only One who could grant him entrance to the kingdom of God, which he sought so desperately. Without repentance and faith, there was no other way into God's kingdom. This was a very heavy pill to swallow. Nicodemus had a lot to ponder.

A Father's Motive

Jesus clearly sensed the heaviness of Nicodemus's heart, so He continued by drawing a contrast in which He explained the Father's real motivation in sending His Son. In Jesus's explanation, He told Nicodemus He was not judging him:

16. *For God so loved the world, that He gave His only begotten Son, that whoever believes in Him should not perish, but have eternal life*
17. *For God did not send the Son into the world to judge the world, but that the world should be saved through Him.*

When John uses the term *world*, most folks think he is referring to all the people in the world. And he is! But he really has more in view than just the people, although the people are his primary focus.

John used this term to refer to the entire created universe (including all the people) that exists in its current "fallen" state. John used the word *kosmos*, from which we get our word *cosmos*. It means the whole of creation. If he wanted to refer to just the people of the world, he would have probably used the word *Anthropos*, which refers, generically, to all people. This becomes clear when you consider Paul's statement in Romans 8:22 that even creation "groans," awaiting the redemption of the sons of men.

The "Green Peace" folks really have things backward here. This whole "Save the Planet" movement will never work. It's not that I am against less pollution—not a bit—but the teaching of scriptures is very clear on the healthy planet issue. The necessary prerequisite for a healthy planet is the redemption of men. Men and women must be changed from the inside out through the power of the gospel before the planet will ever have a chance of being cleaned up. The movement is noble but futile at its core because it tries to address human behavior without addressing human nature first. But I digress.

Three things must have immediately jumped out in Nicodemus's mind with Jesus's comment in verse 16. First, was God's primary motivation for sending Jesus (who Nicodemus recognized as a teacher come from God)[108] love? The reason this thought floats into his mind is because Jesus said He came with a love, not only for God's people (the Jews) but for all the people of the world. Jesus was the physical manifestation of the love of God, and that love extended beyond just the nation of Israel. As the song goes, "Red and yellow, black and white, they are precious in His sight." Nicodemus knew that God loved Israel. God called them "His people." But did God really love everyone, even the Gentiles, as much as He loved Israel? That was a pretty radical concept.

The second thing that jumped into Nicodemus's mind was the phrase *"whoever believes in Him."* It was clear to Nicodemus that Jesus was saying that God loved all of humanity equally. Really? Was He really saying *all* of humanity had equal access to the kingdom of God? Could that possibly be true? It seemed preposterous. Could a "Gentile dog" have just as much access to the kingdom of God as a Pharisee of the Great Sanhedrin? It was no wonder that many of Nicodemus's colleagues thought Jesus's "elevator" didn't exactly go all the way to the top floor!

---

[108] John 3:2

The third thing that jumped into Nicodemus's mind was the phrase *"should not perish, but have eternal life."* What was this "perishing" business all about? Certainly, Nicodemus wasn't "perishing"! Nicodemus believed he was "owed" eternal life because of his commitment and sacrifices, to say nothing of his birth privilege. Jesus seemed to be implying the exact opposite. Was He saying all, even Jews, are going to perish if they don't believe in *Him*? At least it certainly sounded like that to Nicodemus.

In following up with verse 17, Jesus debunks a common misunderstanding that even Nicodemus had. A commonly held belief in the "world" today is that the God of the Old Testament is harsh and judgmental. The God of the New Testament is loving and forgiving. Well, which is it? The truth is, it is both, although, I object somewhat to the idea that God is judgmental. I believe the proper view is that God is just. The very definition of being just requires judgment of wrongdoing. So, God is both loving and just.

The point Jesus makes in verse 17 was that Jesus's purpose in becoming flesh and living among us wasn't to judge us, but to save us. It was His intention from the very beginning to die on a cross that He might pay our debt of sin in full so we could stand before the Father with a clean and clear conscience, *clothed in His righteousness.*[109] But in order for Jesus to accomplish that for you and me, He had to take our sin upon Himself and pay the ultimate sacrifice of death on the cross as our substitute. If we will only accept that substitutionary sacrifice, our sins will be forgiven, and we will have access to the kingdom of God. There is no other way.

And that is the choice that Jesus puts forth next:

18. *He who believes in Him is not judged; he who does not believe has been judged already, because he has not believed in the name of the only begotten Son of God.*

---

[109] 2 Corinthians 5:21

A Simple Choice

The choice is very simple. It's a choice of *remaining* in a state of judgment before God or *removing* yourself from a state of permanent judgement before God. Jesus was pretty clear about this, and I don't think Nicodemus missed the point at all. Jesus was saying that all the world and all the people in it are in a permanent condition of judgment before a holy God. He, the only begotten Son of God, had come to provide a way of escape from that judgment if men would only choose it. I hope this is very clear to you. You *are* in a state of judgment. Do you want out? That is the choice Jesus offers Nicodemus and you!

The way you exercise your choice is not to simply say *yes* or *no*. The way to exercise your choice is either to believe (place your complete trust and faith) in Jesus and what He says and does or not believe in Him and reject what He says, does, and offers. That is the choice.

But let me be as clear as I can here. When Jesus says "believe," He is not talking about mere mental consent. It helps no one to say, "I believe Jesus is the Son of God." For goodness' sake, the devil would even say that. In fact, he knows that to be a fundamental fact. He (the devil) believes that with all his being. That is nothing more than mental consent to a fact.

When Jesus talks about believing in Him, He is talking about repenting for our sin and placing our trust and faith in Him. He means abandoning our own resources and leaning wholly upon His grace. He means submitting to Him as our Lord and Savior. That, the devil would never do.

If you will confess your sin and believe in Him in this sense, you will be saved from the pending judgment of God, and you will have access to the kingdom of God. If you reject the "freedom" Jesus offers, you will simply remain in the current state of eternal damnation you are now in.

Light or Darkness

Jesus goes on to explain the "why" and "how of all this judgement:

19. *And this is the judgment, that the light is come into the world, and men loved the darkness rather than the light; for their deeds were evil.*
20. *For everyone who does evil hates the light, and does not come to the light, lest his deeds should be exposed.*
21. *But he who practices the truth comes to the light, that his deeds may be manifested as having been wrought in God.*

What Jesus is saying in a nutshell is that He didn't *bring* judgment, He simply *revealed* judgment. Light doesn't change anything. It simply reveals what is really there. For example, you may have been told stories about all kinds of things that are up in the dark attic of an old home. When you walk up those creaky stairs and slowly open the door to peek into the attic, you can't see a thing. It is pitch-black in there. So you slowly reach carefully around the doorjamb to feel for the light switch. Anything could grab your hand and jerk you into that black darkness. When your fingers finally find the switch, you flick it on. A light floods the space, chasing the darkness away; absolutely nothing changes in the attic. All the light does is reveal what is really there.

That is exactly what happened when the light of God, His only begotten Son, stepped onto the human scene. Nothing changed. The human scene didn't change. The presence of Jesus simply revealed by contrast the character of the human heart for what it really was. What His life and teaching revealed was that the heart of man was deceitful above all things and exceedingly corrupt, just as the prophet of old had said.[110] When a man compares his life and attitudes with those of

---

[110] Jeremiah 17:9

Jesus's, he automatically sees the ugliness of his own fallen nature. It dawns upon him that his heart is evil. OOPS! That's no good!

Jesus says that men love darkness rather than light because their deeds are evil. Jesus uses the term darkness as a metaphor for the ignorance of divine truth. God has revealed, in contrast to His Son, the true nature of man. Jesus is God's standard of how life is to be lived.

A Great Myth

Here, Jesus exposes one of the greatest myths foisted upon society: the myth that way deep down in the heart of every man there is a spark of good. If we just look hard enough, we will find that spark of good. That's why we need to encourage people so they will become better and more productive citizens. That's why corporal punishment is not effective. We need to retrain, reeducate, rebuild, reengage that spark of good.

Pardon my French, but that is a load of GARBAGE! Jesus is very clear that if we look way deep down in the heart of every man, we will find the same thing every time, and that is a cesspool of evil called sin that only leads to death. There is nothing good down there to retrain, reeducate, rebuild, or reengage. There is no spark of good. It went out at the fall of man in the garden. And that was our inheritance by birth from the first Adam.[111] This is the very concept that the world is ignorant about and continually fights and rejects.

I know it's hard to admit that I'm a sinner at the core of my being. What's hard about it is that I want people to think I'm the nicest guy on the planet. I want people to think I am loving, kind, generous, helpful, and, above all, very intelligent (I'm having the most trouble trying to be convincing about that last one). I want them to think that I always think of others before I think of myself.

The truth is, however, that is all a crock. Yet that is exactly how every one of us paints the "outside" of ourselves. The reality "way

---

[111] 1 Corinthians 15:21–22

deep down inside" is that, first and foremost, we need to look out for number one, *me*. If I don't look out for myself, no one else will. I am the captain of my own ship, the master of my own fate, and the director of my own destiny. So, get out of my way! I've only got one go in this life, and I need to make the most of it.

We all want everyone else to see a positive image of us, but down inside, we all know very clearly there is something quite different. The fact is, I have convinced myself that I am in control of my own life, and I like it that way. I don't want anyone else telling me what to do. The ignorance of divine reality is the fact that God never designed me (or you) to run my life in my own strength or wisdom. I was created by God to be a servant, not a master. As Blaise Pascal, the French philosopher of the midsixteen hundreds, wisely said, "There is a God-shaped vacuum in the heart of every man, which cannot be filled by any created thing, but only by God, the Creator, made known through Jesus." I have placed myself in that "God-shaped vacuum." As Bill Bright, the founder of Campus Crusade for Christ, always put it, "I am seated on the throne of my own life." But that is all wrong. God designed that vacuum at the center of my life to be filled by God Himself, through His Son, Jesus Christ. It's Jesus that needs to be seated on the throne of my life. Not me!

When I am in charge of my life, as long as *I* fill that vacuum with things that *I* think are important, my life will eventually spin out of control. I'll never know the abundant Christian life,[112] the deep satisfaction and inner peace God has designed for me to experience. Once I relinquish the control of my life over to God's Son, Jesus, it is only then that I will begin to realize, for the first time, what life is all about and how God intended it to be lived. Only as I submit every moment of my life to Him will I ever know the peace and purpose God created me to experience. The reason men love darkness rather than light is nothing more than a control issue. They don't want to give the control of their lives over to anyone, including

---

[112] John 10:10

Jesus. They simply want to hide the fact of their own incompetence, ineptitude, and insecurity. They don't want anyone to see that they really aren't in control like they pretend to be.

Two Kinds of People

In verses 21 and 22, Jesus draws a clear distinction between two kinds of people. All people fall into one of these two categories. There are those who "come to the light" and those who "do not come to the light." Jesus is not talking about Christians and non-Christians here. He is simply talking about human behavior.

Those who do not come to the light are defined in verse 20 as those who do evil. Those who come to the light are defined in verse 21 as "those who practice the truth." Jesus goes on to say that the problem with those who do evil is that they don't want their deeds to be exposed; whereas those who practice the truth want their deeds to be "manifest" as being wrought by God.

Let's pick this apart for a moment. By "come to the light," Jesus means to be exposed to the truth of His word. It means to be evaluated by the standard that Jesus has set for all our deeds as demonstrated by His life. (Those who don't want their deeds to be measured by God's standards are simply revealing their "evil" nature.)

Actually, there are two words for *evil* here. The word for evil in verse 19 means that which is full of hardship, difficulties, and annoyances that produce toil and peril, resulting in trouble and pain. In a physical sense, it refers to something that is diseased or blind. In an ethical sense, it means something that is bad or wicked, evil! This describes the "deeds" of those who don't practice the truth.

The word *evil* in verse 20 is a different word but akin to the one in 19. This word in verse 20 means "that which is mean (as in mean-spirited), worthless, or of no account." In an ethical sense, it is the idea of something that is bad or base (in a gross sense). This describes the actions of those who do evil deeds and is why these people hate the light. It is because the light exposes all of this "evil," both in terms of behavior and deeds. They don't want the reality of either their motivations or actions to be exposed, lest people think less of them. They love the approval of men rather than God. I'm not talking about politics here, am I?

The contrast in verse 21 is quite acute. Those who come to the light are those who practice the truth. *Practice* here means "to make, produce, or accomplish; to perform or carry out an act for a definite result." That result is that their deeds may be exposed by the light and be manifest as being "wrought" by God. *Wrought* is the idea of being produced by God. Those who practice the truth want others to take account of what God is doing in and through them. Those who love darkness don't want anyone to know that it is really all about themselves.

The contrast is between those who do deeds in their own strength, effort, and wisdom and those who do deeds that they have allowed God to produce through them. The first group hates the light. The second group seeks out the light. The first group seeks the praise of men. The second group seeks the praise of God. Those who reject the truth of the gospel message will sink deeper and deeper into a spiral of decay and despair. Those who respond to the truth of the gospel will draw closer and closer to the Light Himself.

Enough Said

At this point, as far as we know, the conversation with Nicodemus is concluded. There is no question in my mind that Nicodemus's mind has been blown away. Jesus has both reduced this brilliant scholar to the level of the lowest of men in terms of the requirements for entering God's kingdom and has also lifted him to the heights of the sons of God at the same time.

Nicodemus's heart was filled with pride as *the* teacher of Israel and as a Pharisee who had dedicated his life to pleasing God. He has just learned that all that effort and dedication accounts for nothing in terms of gaining access to the kingdom of God. He has also learned, as a truth seeker, that he stood on the very threshold of the kingdom of God. That which he had spent his entire life seeking was within his grasp.

What a conflicting feeling of dejection and hope must have filled Nicodemus's heart, but it was now plain and simple to him. He had a decision to make. Would he believe this "teacher come from God" and place his complete trust and faith in Him, or would he dismiss Him as nothing more than a heretic of Judaism like many of his colleagues had done?

This is the ultimate challenge Jesus has laid before Nicodemus. It is the same ultimate challenge Jesus lays before every one of us. The question is, is Nicodemus (or are you) going to be a truth-denier and drift back into darkness or continue to be a truth-seeker and allow himself (yourself) to be drawn to the Light? The answer to that question will remain a mystery for the next couple of years. In time, we will discover the path Nicodemus chose. John 19:38–39 reveals the ultimate result of this conversation. We'll revisit Nicodemus later, when we get to that passage.

Application

In the quietness of your bedroom or office tonight, after everyone is gone and you are alone and undisturbed, in the darkness with the lights off, get on your knees beside your bed or office chair. Simply and honestly say to God, "Father, I want to be a 'truth-seeker.' Forgive me my pride and self-centeredness and fill me with the Spirit of your Son. Give me the grace from this moment forward to know the truth and live the truth in a way that will honor you. Amen." Be careful, there are exciting changes ahead!

CHAPTER 10

A Baptizer's Humility
John 3:22-36

This weekend is the Apple Cup! What an exciting game is in store. University of Washington and Washington State University, cross-state rivals, will square off this weekend in Pullman, home turf for WSU. Both are 7–1 in conference play. This is for a Pac-12 north conference title and a chance to move up in the national ranking. Prestigious bowl bids are on the line. GO, COUGS!

Competition is an exciting component to any athletic sport. Carol and I have sat many a time in Martin Stadium on the campus of WSU to watch the Washington State Cougars battle opponents from all over the country. The excitement is electrifying both before and during the game, and we aren't even alumni.

However, when it comes to the church, competition is not only an awkward idea, but it can be both ugly and messy. Yet amazingly, churches do compete and even brag about who is better than the other. As we approach this next section, we run into John the Baptist again. This is the last time we will hear from him in John's gospel. It is John the Baptist's final testimony as the forerunner of Jesus. In this passage, we will see that the issue of competition was alive, even in Jesus's day, as it is today in far too many Christian circles.

Let's begin by reading John 3:22–24:

22. *After these things Jesus and His disciples came into the land of Judea, and there He was spending time with them and baptizing.*
23. *John also was baptizing in Aenon near Salim, because there was much water there; and people were coming and were being baptized.*
24. *For John had not yet been thrown into prison.*

A Model of Discipleship

The passage begins with Jesus extending His ministry into Judea, bringing along His disciples. We are told that Jesus was "spending time" with His disciples. It is interesting to me that John puts it so casually. Most of us normally think of spending time with friends as just hanging out together. You know, quality time, having a beer (or iced tea), watching the Seahawks, laughing, and catching up with one another.

But I don't think that is the kind of "hanging out" or "spending time together" John is talking about here. John tells us they were "baptizing." (Now there's a different definition of "spending time together.") Baptizing implies more than just dunking some folks in the water. This partially explains why they were somewhere in the area of Aenon near Salim. The Jordan River ran nearby. It was the perfect place if you wanted to baptize some folks. Here, Jesus was giving His men some "hands-on" experience in ministry. This is a classic example of Jesus's method of discipleship.

This was one of the disciples' first real experiences in being a witness for the Master. This was real-time hands-on training. It must have seemed quite remarkable to the disciples that Jesus asked them to baptize those in the crowd that were willing to openly repent for their sin. That was usually the responsibility of only the important people, like the priests or Pharisees or John the Baptist. This wasn't something a common person should be doing. These guys were only fishermen, for goodness' sake.

Jesus was showing his disciples that baptizing converts and helping them become followers of the Messiah was everyone's responsibility. This is how Jesus was "spending time" or "hanging out" with his disciples. He was sharing the responsibility of ministry and involving them in it. I would suggest that there is no better bonding agent for any two or more believers than to share in some ministry experience together.

I love to fly-fish with friends. For me, that is a great bonding experience. But recently, Carol and I took a trip to San Jose to spend some time with some folks who were in our high school Sunday school class as students back in the early '70s. These were kids in whom we had invested a huge portion of our lives and time. They were kids we spent months training to share the gospel and teach vacation Bible school classes. After months of training, we would take them into some small rural towns in Western Nevada for a week at a time to run vacation Bible schools, all on their own, with only one adult there to supervise.

These are kids who are now grown adults with families of their own. It was four decades ago that we were involved with them. Yet those mutually shared ministry experiences have produced relationships that don't hold a candle to the friendships I have with my fly-fishing friends. Nothing draws you closer in a relationship than sharing in ministry together. That is what Jesus was doing in Judea. It's called discipleship.

Same Message?

Baptizing implies that there was some kind of following that Jesus and His disciples had developed. Further, it implies that they were preaching a message similar to John's message, a message of repenting for sins that needed to be publicly declared by the ritual of water baptism. It identified the follower as being symbolically cleansed. According to verse 26, later on in the text, their ministry must have been quite successful. The text tells us "all are coming to Him." It would appear that Jesus was "outbaptizing" John the Baptist. A legitimate question arises here. "Was the message of Jesus any different from the message of John?" The answer to that is *yes* and *no*.

In one respect, their messages were identical. According to Mark 1:15, Jesus was preaching the necessity for repenting for sin and demonstrating that obedience through the symbolic act of water baptism—same as John. However, Jesus added a very important caveat to His message. He included the concept "*and* believe in the gospel." It would seem odd to us that Jesus would be preaching, "believe in the gospel." Most conservative Christians believe the gospel is defined by the Apostle Paul in 1 Corinthians 15:1–4 as Christ died for our sins, was buried, and that He was raised from the dead on the third day. Well, certainly, none of that had happened yet. So Jesus couldn't be preaching that message, could He? Was this some different gospel? I hope not, because Paul tells us in Galatians 1:8–9 that if anyone preached a gospel other than the one God had given to Paul, *"let him be accursed."*

I think this issue can easily be resolved by simply understanding the term *gospel* for what it really means, "good news." The good news Jesus was preaching was that the Messiah had come. The One the nation had long expected had now arrived on the scene. He was the One who had come in fulfillment of all prophecies of the Old Testament. He was the Lamb of God who had come, as John had said, to take away the sins of the world.[113] The Messiah had stepped into a dark and dreary scene with a message of hope. Now, having repented for their sin, people were to place their faith, hope, and trust in Him as their Savior. He was the One *who would* give Himself as a sacrifice for our sins. That is what Jesus added to His message that was different from John.

---

[113] John 1:29

Allow me a slight diversion here. The declaration by John that Jesus was the "Lamb of God who takes away the sin of the world" was a remarkable claim. The Baptizer knew exactly what he was saying when he made that comment about Jesus. But it must have been very confusing to the Jews. The association of a lamb being a sacrificial substitute for sin was obvious. Regularly in the temple folks brought their sacrificial lambs as sacrifices for their sins. As the priest slit the throat of the lamb, the sinner would place his hand on the lamb as a symbolic act of transferring his sins to the lamb. As the blood was shed and the lamb died, the sinner's sins died with the lamb. The lambs blood had washed away the sin. This was a common understanding.

John was saying that God was providing a sacrificial lamb, not for God's sins, but for the sins *of the world*. And the lamb John was pointing to was Jesus. The implication was two-fold. First, Jesus was pure, spotless, without blemish and sinless. We will see later that this is an oxymoron for the Jews. Jesus couldn't be sinless or blameless. He worked on the Sabbath, for goodness sake, in direct violation of one of the basic Ten Commandments!

Second, it implied that Jesus was to be sacrificed for the whole world. Besides the fact that men were never sacrificed in the temple (what a horrid thought), that was an oxymoron itself. If He was truly the Messiah as the Baptizer seemed to believe, how could He set up His kingdom and rule over Israel if He was going to be sacrificed? John's claim about Jesus just didn't make logical, rational sense. This logic by the Jews will come to a head in chapter 5.

There is one other observation I want to make. In Acts 1:8, in one of Jesus's postresurrection appearances, Jesus instructed His disciples on how the gospel message was to spread. "After I am gone," He said, *"you shall receive power when the Holy Spirit comes upon you; and you shall be My witnesses both in Jerusalem, and in all Judea and Samaria, and even to the remotest part of the earth."*

Clearly, there is a progression here: Jerusalem, Judea, Samaria, and the remotest part of the earth. As we go through John's gospel, we will discover that the first place Jesus shared the gospel was in Jerusalem with Nicodemus, the Pharisee of the Jews. He is now preaching and baptizing in Judea, around Aenon near Salim. Next, in chapter 4, He will move to Samaria with the woman at the well. And when we get there, we will see that the next stop in Jesus's ministry is the remotest part of the earth! Just watch!

Do you see how the Son of Man is modeling what He will tell His men to do?

Trouble Arises

In verse 23, John is also carrying on his ministry of baptizing in the same area, in Aenon near Salim. Many were still coming to John. Apparently, John and Jesus were in proximity. Some commentators believe they were only about three or four miles apart at this time. As we've mentioned, their messages were almost identical. Both were preaching the necessity of repentance.

Our author gives us a time reference in verse 24, *"John had not yet been thrown in prison."* We are given this reference to show that the time of John's ministry is about to end. This helps us to understand that the necessity for the disciples of John to transfer their allegiance to Jesus must soon take place. That is what God intended, and that's what John expected. John's ministry was designed from the beginning to be preparatory. His job was to "get the ball rolling, then pass it off to Jesus." It was never in John's mind to establish a "lasting" ministry. Still, John's ministry is not yet over. When it is, God will bring it to an end. The same is true for each one of us.

As I mentioned at our life group last Sunday night, if you wake up in the morning and you are still breathing, God still has a purpose for your earthly existence. The morning, you wake up and you're not breathing, that's the morning He will be finished with your usefulness, and you will go home to be with Him for all eternity.

Well, here comes trouble:

25. *Therefore there arose a discussion on the part of John's disciples with a Jew about purification.*
26. *And they came to John and said to him, "Rabbi, He who was with you beyond the Jordan, to whom you have testified, behold, He is baptizing and all are coming to Him."*

Verse 25 reveals to us that a discussion arose between the disciples of John and some Jew about purification, that is to say, baptism. Baptism was a symbol of purification for sins. Most likely, this Jew the disciples of John were talking to was someone who had been baptized by Jesus. I'm sure they questioned this Jew as to *why* he had been baptized by Jesus when John was the "original" baptizer.

Apparently, the discussion didn't end satisfactorily for John's disciples, so they brought the issue to John for some clarification. It seems that the sticky point was the fact that Jesus was baptizing *more people* than John. The offense was most likely that John was the senior member when it came to this ministry of baptizing and Jesus was the newcomer on the block. After all, it was John who gave Jesus His start. John had "borne witness" of Jesus, giving Him free advertisement. All Jerusalem and Judea were coming out to be baptized by John. This endorsement by John of Jesus was great publicity for Jesus. Folks wouldn't have known who Jesus was had it not been for John.

In addition, Jesus had been with John. Jesus had been part of John's crowd, listening to John's message. And eventually, Jesus went forward to be baptized by John, surely identifying Himself as one of John's disciples. And now He's competing with John! There's real gratitude for you.

Jesus was considered to be undermining John's ministry. John had the copyrights, and Jesus was plagiarizing what John invented. He might have put a little bit of a twist on it, "Believe in the gospel," but baptizing for repentance was John's idea. Let's face it; Jesus was nothing more than John's protégé. And now He's copying John and doing so just down the street! What is this, church row?

This was the thinking of John's disciples. The point is, John was here first. John established this ministry *before* Jesus came along. And here is Jesus in the same area, horning in. Any way you slice it, this was offensive to the disciples of John. This was a big area, Judea. Jesus needed to go somewhere else. John had first rights! These were the feelings of John's disciples. They were offended for John. It was all about competition, jealousy, and pride.

Comparing Ministries

Comparing ministries to determine who is better or bigger drives me nuts and is the ultimate insult to God. When I was in professional ministry, our pastoral staff went to pastors' conferences every year. It was always a great time of bonding for our team. But the thing that always drove me crazy about pastors when they got together was that the conversation around the dinner table inevitably turned to "How big is your congregation?" "How many souls has your church saved this past year?" and "How big is your mission's budget?"

The conversation was always about "*my* church," "*my* souls," "*my* missions budget." I had always thought it was Christ's church, His souls, and His budget. Wow! Had I ever been confused! You could smell the pride around the tables as pastors bragged about size, money, and scalps.

In the ten years I was a college and high school pastor in San Jose, there was a youth pastor from a local megachurch that I used to meet with regularly on the campus of San Jose State College. We would meet to pray for the college and high school kids we were working with on the campus and in the high schools. Every time we met, he would always brag about how much his churches' mission's budget had grown and the hundreds of students in his ministry. I'm not sure why he felt he had to impress me with his ministry.

Not long after I came to Spokane to start a church, there was a pastor of a church here in town that placed an ad in the local paper that he would give $10 to the first one hundred people that came to his church the next Sunday morning. He actually did that! I guess the attraction of the church was the gospel plus $10! His sermon that Sunday morning, so I was told, was on tithing. I suppose he hoped that those first one hundred people would put their $10 bill back in the offering. It's a good thing I was busy that Sunday morning or I'd be $10 richer! Competition among churches can be sickening.

Same Baptism?

In this passage, John's and Jesus's baptisms were identical. But is this the same picture of Christian baptism that we practice today? Of course not. Paul changes the picture in Romans 6:3–5. Today, post-resurrection, the picture of Christian baptism is one of identification, symbolically, with the death, burial, *and* resurrection of Jesus. It's a personal public testimony that the one being baptized is identifying with the fact that Jesus died for their sin, that He was buried and took those sins with Him to the grave, and that He was raised from the dead so that they too would be raised with Him to walk in newness of life. It is a declaration to all that they have been set free from the bondage and enslavement of sin.

The basic difference between the baptism of John and Jesus, and Christian baptism today, is that the baptisms of John and Jesus symbolized the need to have hearts cleansed through confession and repentance as a precursor to being filled with His Spirit. Obviously, the filling of the Holy Spirit would not come until Pentecost. They looked forward to the gospel event that would solve the sin problem, which was the death, burial, and resurrection of Jesus. We look back to that same event. Christian baptism today symbolizes and celebrates everything the baptism of John or Jesus looked forward to. Our baptism celebrates the gospel events as accomplished facts.

The reason for Jesus's greater success is relatively obvious. Not only was His message more complete, "Repent *and* believe in the gospel," but John had already endorsed Jesus as being superior to him. John had denied he was the Messiah to the Pharisaic Inquisition Team.[114] Jesus was freely using the title *Son of God*, which was a Messianic title. And Jesus was authenticating His claims as Messiah through the signs He was doing. John did no signs because John was not the Messiah.

Clearly John's disciples loved him and didn't like to see him getting beat in his own backyard, but John's disciples were totally misguided and had lost the real focus of what John was all about. It was never John's goal from the start to "outdo" Jesus. In fact, quite the opposite. John's ministry was to shine a light on Jesus's ministry. His goal was to point to it, call attention to it, to prepare folks to follow Jesus, not himself. John always understood that God had appointed him as a reed blowing in the wilderness.[115] He was never to be the focus of attention. Would that more folks in professional ministry had John's attitude today. The focus should never be on us but on the One we have been placed on this earth to serve, Jesus the Messiah!

Not My Ministry

I often hear folks refer to the Sunday school class I teach as *my* ministry or *my* Sunday school class. I understand the need to identify the class as distinct from another Sunday school class, and that doesn't bother me, but that term "my Sunday school class" always gives me a subtle reminder that I would not even have the privilege of ministry if God had not allowed it. It's *His* class and not mine. He's given me some responsibility with it, but He hasn't given me ownership of it. It is His ministry, designed by Him for His glory. I am nothing more than the tool He has chosen to use at this moment.

---

[114] John 1:19–24
[115] Matthew 11:7

I love our teaching pastor, Ben. He's a great teacher. He's a compassionate elder. He's a wise shepherd. But Valley Bible Church isn't about Ben in any way, shape, or form, and there's no doubt in my mind that Ben would agree. This church is about Jesus. It's about the message Ben preaches. It's about the gospel and reaching this community for Christ.

"I am of Ben" is a deadly sin that we all must avoid that can be seen in so many of our churches today. The beginning of this sin can be seen when we refer to Valley Bible Church as "Ben's church." This may sound like splitting hairs, but usually, it winds up splitting churches. This is Jesus's church. We are His body. Don't ever confuse the mission of your church with its leadership. John's followers were upset because they thought Jesus was hurting John's ministry. It was never John's ministry. It was always God's ministry that He had appointed John to lead. Big difference.

This is a huge problem in most churches today. Unfortunately, the contemporary thinking in most churches is, "Let's get a super charismatic pastor so our church will really grow. Then we will be more successful than those other churches in town." Good grief!

The Reason for Success

John's response to this is very revealing:

27. *John answered and said, "A man can receive nothing unless it has been given him from heaven.*
28. *"You yourselves are my witnesses that I said, 'I am not the Christ,' but, 'I have been sent ahead of Him.'"*

John obviously understood where success in any ministry came from. It came from heaven. God was the one who gave and blessed ministry. No one else. It was not the result of charismatic preachers, dynamic worship services, "March to Sunday school in March" campaigns, or any amount of clever marketing. Success in ministry comes from heaven based on faith. It cannot be measured by size, finances, or the number of buses a church owns.

John understood he had no control over how many were coming to him to be baptized. If God had sent only one person to be baptized by John, he would have considered that to be a success. John didn't earn his success. He didn't deserve his success. His success wasn't based on any merit of its own. It was God who chose him for the ministry he had. John's mind was clear, "Every good and perfect gift comes down from above" (James 1:17)

Do you realize how dynamic the influence in our communities would be if every pastor of every church would adopt the Baptizer's point of view? An attitude that, though we work very hard, everything we accomplish, all our great achievements, are simply gifts from God. We are not "self-made" men. All that we have or will ever accomplish comes from His gracious hand. The problem is, dealing with ego is a messy and difficult business.

Just think about it for a moment. Our greatest blessings really have nothing to do with our "material success." Because of what Jesus did on the cross on our behalf, we have peace with God, the gift of eternal life, the forgiveness of our sin, a place prepared for us in heaven, grace sufficient to meet every need, wisdom from above for every difficulty, and God's Spirit without measure. All these come as a gift of God's love and grace. This is what John is saying. This is the real measure of success.

Know Your Place

John also realized his limitation. He was not the Christ. He was not God. He was only one sent, the messenger, the servant of Messiah. He did not deserve, nor was he worthy of… what belongs to Jesus. John knew and understood his place:

29. *He who has the bride is the bridegroom; but the friend of the bridegroom, who stands and hears him, rejoices greatly because of the bridegroom's voice. So this joy of mine has been made full.*

John was completely comfortable with how he fit into the will and plan of God. He knew he was a "groomsman," he was not the bridegroom. He was a friend of the bridegroom, the best man, the one who served the groom. John was constantly listening for the voice of the groom so he could respond when needed. He rejoiced when he heard the bridegroom calling him because he knew there was something he could do to serve and please the bridegroom.

Do you know your place in relation to the "bridegroom"? Often, believers get caught in the trap of thinking that Jesus saved us to serve us, but that isn't exactly how His kingdom works. Christianity or ministry isn't about *you*. It has always been, and it will always be, about Him. The very reason He called you out of darkness into His marvelous light was so you would be an ambassador for Him. He gifted you to enable you to serve Him. He has called you to be light and salt in the world for His glory. You are to be His witnesses. How often we see good people in positions of ministry who act (and I would assume, think) that their ministry is all about them?

John the Baptist was completely secure in who he was, why he was here, and what he was doing. Because he understood his position, he was completely comfortable with the only conclusion that made any sense to him as we see in verse 30. If you were ever looking for a "life verse" for your own personal ministry, here it is:

30. *He must increase, but I must decrease.*

It was no surprise to John that Jesus was "baptizing, and all were coming to Him." That's the way things were supposed to work. He must increase. John must decrease. John understood that all glory, honor, and power belong to Jesus. The very fact that Jesus's ministry was increasing and John's ministry was decreasing was the mark of success John was looking for. To the degree that any of us in ministry receive the credit and glory is the degree to which we have failed.

The difficult reality is that our most ardent supporters can become our greatest problem. We know they love us and we are very encouraged by that love. But all the handshaking, pats on the back, and the accolades can play havoc with our ego. The last thing we need is to subtly begin to believe that "we really did do a good job. God is sure lucky to have me on His side." That is deadly.

In the church I grew up in, it was the pastor's job at the end of every service to go to the back of the church at the end of the sermon and greet the folks as they left. In fact, in the very first church where I served as teaching pastor, that's what was expected of me. But as I observed my old pastor at the church door greeting people as they left, it became clear that it was too much "Good job, Pastor." "You hit the nail on the head today." "I was really moved." "You are a blessing to us." "Where do you get all those insights?" Are these comments of encouragement helpful or hurtful? That's a hard question. Pastors need to be encouraged, so how do you do that without inflating their ego? I don't have a good answer, but I think your praise needs to be short and sweet. I think the pastor's acknowledgment needs to be limited to "Thank you."

When I first attended Peninsula Bible Church as a college student, I was immediately struck by the fact that Ray Stedman never went to the back of the church to greet people as they left. I finally asked him why he didn't do that. His answer was short and clear. "It's not good for my ego." The Baptizer had the same attitude. "He must increase, I must decrease." What a great slogan for the office wall of every pastor.

Closing Summation

In verses 31–36, John tells us exactly why He must increase and we must decrease:

31. *He who comes from above is above all, he who is of the earth is from the earth and speaks of the earth. He who comes from heaven is above all.*
32. *What He has seen and heard, of that He testifies; and no one receives His testimony.*

33. *He who has received His testimony has set his seal to this, that God is true.*
34. *For He whom God has sent speaks the words of God; for He gives the Spirit without measure.*
35. *The Father loves the Son and has given all things into His hand.*
36. *He who believes in the Son has eternal life; but he who does not obey the Son will not see life, but the wrath of God abides on him.*

This last paragraph of chapter 3 is John the Baptist's last statement about Jesus. It is a summation of everything John had said about Jesus. He began by sharing with us two unique perspectives Jesus had. The first is in verse 31.

Have you ever been in the back of a large crowd of people trying to see what is going on up front? Or have your ever been to the Rose Parade in Pasadena where tens of thousands line the streets to see the parade and you are about ten to fifteen people back from the front?

What do you have to do to get a good view of the parade? If you've been there, all you have to do is look around. There are people standing on their tiptoes. Others are sitting on large blue mailboxes. Some are standing on fire hydrants. Several are perched in trees. If you have a few extra bucks, you can get a seat in one of the many bleachers that are set up along the parade route. The reason people seek these elevated positions is obvious. They can get a better view of what's going on and what's coming ahead.

That is exactly what John is saying about Jesus in verse 31. Jesus comes from an elevated position. He *"comes from above."* When Jesus speaks, He speaks from a context of being able to see the whole picture. He can easily look across the expanse of all of human history, from the beginning to the very end. Therefore His perspective encompasses the whole of truth. He sees the whole parade at one time.

Those of us from earth can only see from our limited perspective. We peer through the crowd, and there it is! The Disney float!

But that is the only thing we can see. Then we hear the roar of the crowd and the cheers. We don't know exactly the reason they are cheering. We have to wait for the next float to come by in order to see why they are cheering. We just don't have the big picture clearly in view. That's what John is saying. Jesus is above all. He can see how it all fits together and tells it like it really is.

Many Christians, and almost all non-Christians, are critical of God about the existence of evil in the world. Why does God allow ISIS to slaughter innocent Christians? Why doesn't God do something about the innocent who suffer? I have seen Facebook postings of people saying they've lost their faith in God because Trump was elected president! If someone's faith is contingent upon an election, I'm not sure I'd want to be in his or her shoes at the Second Coming.

Our problem is that we can only see what's going on from our very limited perspective. We see things in a snippet of time. God sees what's going from the beginning to the very end. He knows where this is all going to lead. He has the situation clearly in His hands. We just need to learn to trust His perspective and quit judging from our limited perspective.

There is another unique perspective that Jesus has in verse 32. When you say to someone, "I'm telling you what I've seen and heard," what are you actually saying? You are telling them you were an eyewitness of the event. You are saying you were there, you personally saw it, you personally heard it. That is what John is saying about Jesus. Jesus is *not* offering us secondhand truth or hearsay knowledge. Not only does Jesus have a better advantage to see the truth, He speaks from personal experience. It is obvious to John why *"all are coming to Him."*[116]

Then John says something interesting in the above passage. He says, *"No man receives His witness"* then immediately says, *"He who has received His witness."* What kind of sense does that make? With his first statement, John is affirming what Paul would later write in

---

[116] John 3:26

Romans 3 (and what David said in Psalms 14 and 53) that *"there is none righteous, not even one. There are none who understand, there is none who seeks for God. All men have turned aside, together they have become useless; There is none who does good, there is not even one. Their throat is an open grave, With their tongues they keep deceiving, The poison of asps is under their lips."*[117] No man receives God's witness, Jesus, unless God grabs his attention.

The good news is that God is constantly at work, seeking to grab man's attention. Those who choose to believe what Jesus is saying as truth, John says, are setting their seal to the fact that God is truth. This means they are staking their very lives on that fact. They are putting their trust and faith in the reality that God is truth and has revealed that truth in Jesus Christ.

The Baptizer affirms what the Apostle John states in chapter 1 verse 14 of this gospel that God's word *"became flesh and dwelt among us."*[118] His name was Jesus. Jesus was God's premier form of communication with men. We will see later on in this gospel that every single word that came out of the mouth of Jesus was what the Father had Him speak. He spoke the very words of God, literally.

He proved His words were God's words by the very signs He did. He spoke the word and the lame walked. He spoke the word and the blind saw. He spoke the word and the sick were healed. He spoke the word and the dead were raised. Jesus gave the Spirit without measure to all those He touched, and He will give the Spirit without measure to you if you will receive His touch by faith.

How can Jesus do all that? On what authority does Jesus have the right to give us God's Spirit? John tells us in verse 35. He can do it because the Father has given all things into His hands. The Father loves and trusts the Son. The Father and the Son are one in essence and purpose. Jesus Himself will openly declare, *"I and the Father are one."*[119] Therefore, the Father has given all things into the Son's

---

[117] Romans 3:10–13
[118] John 1:14
[119] John 10:30

hands. The Son is in complete control and has complete authority to give the Spirit without measure.

Your Choice

The Baptizer ends his comments about Jesus with an ominous choice in verse 36. Either you believe in the Son and are willing to place your faith and trust in Him, for which God will give you eternal life, or you do not believe in God's Son, for which God will deny you eternal life and instead will let His wrath abide on you. A clear choice!

Many folks are confused about what eternal life really is. Most think it is living forever. But it can't be that. Everyone lives forever. Whether you are a believer in Jesus or not, you will live forever. One of the biggest lies foisted upon man is that at death, life is over. It is not. Death is not a wall but an open door, and the choices we make in this life determine what door we will walk through at death.

In every place the term *eternal life* is used in the Bible, it is used to describe "quality" of life, not "quantity" of life. Jesus sums up in a phrase what eternal life is in His high priestly prayer in John 17 as "knowing the Father."[120] Knowing the Father manifests itself in many ways in our existential life on earth. Knowing the Father is experienced when we realize our sins have been forgiven. With that comes freedom from guilt, shame, confusion, fear, loneliness, and doubt. All that is replaced with hope, anticipation, direction, clarity, joy, love, peace. Eternal life is a life filled with the fruit of the Spirit. It is a life of grace without measure, a life of sufficient power within, provided by the grace of God, to meet all the pressures of life without. The frosting on the cake is a life of fellowship in the presence of Jesus for all eternity.

If you don't obey (or believe) the Son, there are two consequences. First, John says, you will not see life. You will never know

---

[120] John 17:3

all that this life has to offer. You will be left to face the harsh realities of life in your own strength. None of God's resources will be available to you. You will be stuck in your misery, and life will crush in around you. Hopelessness, fear, and anxiety will be around every turn in life, and they will wear you down.

In addition, the wrath of God will abide on you. God's wrath is life without Him. Not only your earthly existence but your eternal future will be without God. The ultimate outcome will result in being cast into an outer darkness that will be filled with depression, misery, and fear because that is what life without God really is.

God did not create you to live life apart from Him. He designed you to be a vessel that would contain Him. A vessel that is filled with anything else, or one not filled at all, faces a hopeless, miserable future. Don't be that person.

Application

God didn't save you because He needed you to accomplish His mission and purpose on earth. He didn't save you because you could make His job much easier with all your talent and wisdom. He didn't save you because you would be such a great asset to Him. He saved you because He loved you, and if He hadn't saved you, you would have been lost for all eternity, without hope, and without ever knowing real life.

The next time you are called on to do anything for the cause of Christ, whether it is witness to a friend, serve as an usher at church, take a meal to a sick brother or sister, stop before you do it and simply and humbly ask God to honor this simple prayer, "Lord, in this task I'm about to do, would you be magnified and I be unnoticed completely?" Then you'll experience the heart of a true servant of the Lord.

CHAPTER 11

A Divine Appointment (Part 1)
John 4:1-18

Often you may hear Christians talking about events that have happened to them, usually an encounter with another person they didn't expect to run in to, as a "divine appointment." What they mean by that phrase is that God arranged the encounter and it was one that was completely unexpected or unanticipated. It wasn't anything that they planned or designed or set up. Usually, the result of that meeting was enriching in one way or another.

Many Christians that are familiar with the story of the woman at the well feel it was a "divine appointment." They say that, but they really don't believe that. At least not in the sense that I just described above. Most folks think that Jesus knew exactly what was going to happen at Jacob's well in Samaria. In fact, they will say, the proof of that is the text which says Jesus *had to go through Samaria.* He "had" to go because He knew He would meet the woman at the well. Jesus knew this ahead of time. Isn't that how you've understood this story? If this were true, it would have been a divine appointment for the woman, but certainly not for Jesus. For Jesus, it would have been just another appointment in His busy schedule.

But wait a minute! I don't think Jesus had any idea what awaited Him at Jacob's well. From my point of view, this encounter with the woman at the well was a real, genuine "divine appointment," not just for the woman at the well but for Jesus also. Neither had any expectation of the events that were about to unfold that day in Samaria. Here, then, is a perfect illustration of what makes the Christian life so dynamic and exciting.

Needed Separation

It had become obvious to Jesus that the Pharisees were making a big deal of the fact that Jesus was baptizing more disciples than John. The comparison arose because their ministries were so geographically close, near the Jordan River in Aenon.[121] This gave the Pharisees "fodder" to criticize John's ministry. There's no indication of this, but given the events that were soon to begin developing in the book of John, I believe the Pharisees were seeking to turn John against Jesus. Because of this, out of respect and love for John, Jesus decided to head back north. We pick up the text in John 4:1–4:

1. *Therefore when the Lord knew that the Pharisees had heard that Jesus was making and baptizing more disciples than John*
2. *(although Jesus Himself was not baptizing, but His disciples were),*
3. *He left Judea and went away again into Galilee.*
4. *And He had to pass through Samaria.*

Jesus and John were both making and baptizing disciples. A disciple is nothing more than a learner or follower. It's helpful to realize that a disciple is not necessarily a "believer" in the sense that we think of a "believer" as one who has placed their faith and trust in God. Generally, the context will reveal which disciples are believers and which are not. For example, we will see very plainly in our study of John that Judas the betrayer was a disciple of Jesus. He was even one

---

[121] John 3:23

of the selected twelve. But clearly, he was never a believer as described above. Was he a learner? Yes. Was he a follower of Jesus? Yes, physically, not spiritually. He never placed his trust and faith in Jesus. He was not a believer. We'll prove that later in our series.

John's ministry had peaked with a fairly substantial following. All of Jerusalem and Judea were going out into the wilderness to listen to him.[122] From any human account, you would say this was a sign of John's great success in his ministry; but the reality is, the large multitudes John drew were not a sign of his success at all.

John's mission, his ministry, was never to gather a large crowd or a large following. In fact, it was quite the opposite. His mission was to make straight the way of the Lord. It was his job to prepare the way for men to meet and follow the Master. His goal was to get as many as possible ready to follow Jesus. The fact that Jesus was making more disciples than John was the real sign of John's success! By this time in John's ministry, his numbers began to decline. From John's point of view, the more that left him and followed Jesus, the more successful he was.

Here, in my humble opinion, is the job description and pattern of every pastor on the planet. Is it not true that the secret dream of every young pastor is to be the best, most charismatic, and dynamic pastor in town and to have the largest, most successful ministry in town? I will admit, that kind of ambition and drive sounds exciting and positive. But there must be something more than just being "bigger and better." That's the goal of every retail business in town. Is the church just another retail business?

It seems to me the real goal of the local church needs to be more in line with the vision of John the Baptist. That would be a goal of not how big we are, but how many of those that identify with our ministry are becoming faithful followers of Jesus. Is it not the job of the pastor to prepare the folks God gives him, his flock, to meet the Lord and become a willing and obedient follower of Him? Wouldn't

---

[122] Mark 1:5

it be amazing if more men in professional ministry could genuinely rejoice, not that their ministry was getting bigger and bigger but that more were turning to follow Jesus?

It would be fascinating to crawl into the mind of Jesus to see exactly what He was thinking when He decided to leave the area and go back to Galilee. The feeling one gets from the text is that He was showing deference to John. The suggestion is that His proximity was causing confusion in the minds of John's disciples and giving reasons for the Pharisees to pressure John. However, Jesus says in John 5:19, 30 that everything He does, He does because the Father has shown Him to do it. If that is true, the Father must have told Him to move back up north.

The writer makes the point in verse 2 that Jesus, Himself, isn't baptizing; only his disciples are doing that. Jesus wasn't interested in starting a "cult-like" following. Can you imagine the sense of superiority those who had been baptized by Jesus might have had? Here was an opportunity for Jesus to give His disciples some real ministry training and experience.

Samaritans!

The text tells us in verse 4 that Jesus _had_ to go through Samaria. My issue here is not the necessity but the motivation or reason. Any "good" Jew would never have gone to Galilee via the west side of the Jordan, through Samaria. Pious Jews chose the route east of the Jordan River, crossing back over as they neared the Sea of Galilee, to the western side. It would have taken Jesus two days more in travel time and on a much dustier, hotter, and dangerous route to go the "right way," but He would have avoided Samaria altogether. The Jews hated the Samaritans and thus endured the longer journey.

Four hundred fifty years earlier, the Assyrians had conquered the Jews and deported many of them from Samaria (which is now called the West Bank) into other parts of the Assyrian empire. In their place, they brought in foreigners, Gentiles. The "outsiders" also brought along all their pagan religious practices. Those that were brought in from distant regions intermingled and intermarried with the Jews that remained. The resulting mixed-race people were half Jew–half Gentile. After their return from the captivity, the Jews in Jerusalem refused to allow them to take part with them in rebuilding the temple because they had intermarried with other races. These were the Samaritans. Hence, there sprang up an open enmity between the Jews and the Samaritans.

In Jesus's day, the Samaritans accepted only the first five books of Moses. They rejected all the rest of the Old Testament writings. They also intermingled some of their pagan religious practices with some of the Jewish practices. In addition, they built their own temple in Samaria on Mount Gerizim so they wouldn't have to go to the temple in Jerusalem for the required feasts. That was a complete outrage to the orthodox Jews.

Consequently, they were hated by the Jews as a cult and a bunch of heretics. Good, conservative Jews would have nothing to do with them. They were so hated that they wouldn't even cross their territory to get to Galilee. The alternate route, east of the Jordan, became the preferential route.

Jesus Had To

The phrase in verse 4 that says Jesus "*had to*" (go through Samaria) is translated in other versions as "must" or "needed." The term *had* literally means "it is necessary, there is need of, it behooves, is right and proper. " *Had* is a very good translation. My question is, "Why did He have to?" The truth is, the Father directed Him to go through Samaria and that is why he *had* to. The Father told Him to. I would further suggest that at this time, Jesus had absolutely no idea what awaited Him at Jacob's well any more than you have any idea what awaits you when you go shopping at Safeway today. In obedient expectation, Jesus and His men head north to Galilee, through Samaria, not knowing what awaited them at the well.

In doing so, Jesus cuts right across all kinds of racial prejudice, social superiority, and class differences for all time and for all generations. Here, the disciples are going to learn some life-changing truths about how they are to view those they instinctively don't like and about whom they think are of a lower status than themselves. This is going to be a huge object lesson in "racial equality."

I love this because (in my opinion) Jesus had no idea whatsoever that He was going to run into a woman at a well. Jesus did not look into the future and see this woman coming to the well and then decide to go meet her. No! Jesus had emptied Himself of that privilege of deity. He couldn't look into the future and see what lay ahead any more than you or I can. That is what Paul says in Philippians 2. The Father told Him to head up to Galilee through Samaria. That's *why* He had to go through Samaria.

The Setting

As things turned out, they got to Samaria about suppertime. They were all tired and thirsty when they stopped at the well. So, Jesus sent the boys into town to McDonalds with a "to-go" order. They would probably spend the night near the well and head on into Galilee in the morning. Jesus had absolutely no idea this woman was going to show up. But here she came, right on cue, directed by the Father. Jesus picked up on the opportunity in a New York second! (A New York second is standardized by the time between the lights turning green and the taxi behind you starts beeping his horn).[123] It began to become clear to Jesus why the Father had instructed Him to go through Samaria.

That's how the Christian life is to be lived, in complete obedience to the Father, with a great sense of expectation for what the Father might dump right in your lap. That is exactly the subpoint to this whole "woman at the well" story.

---

[123] *Urbandictionary.com*

The scene began to develop:

5. *So He came to a city of Samaria called Sychar, near the parcel of ground that Jacob gave to his son Joseph;*
6. *and Jacob's well was there. So Jesus, being wearied from His journey, was sitting thus by the well. It was about the sixth hour.*
7. *There came a woman of Samaria to draw water.*

Notice that John identifies the exact location of this well, the plot of land the well is on, and the time of day. This was all located in the valley of Shechem that lies between Mount Ebal and Mount Gerizim. This was where the nation gathered for the curses and blessings back in Joshua's day. After Israel's defeat of Jericho, Bethel, and Ai, during the time of the conquest under Joshua, it was here the whole nation gathered. Here, God laid before the people of Israel the requirement to choose either blessings for obedience or curses for disobedience. It was a place of choosing life or death. It was here God challenged His own people to choose to either follow Him fully and be blessed or to choose to go their own path in life and be cursed. And that is exactly what this scene is all about. Jesus knows all this, and here comes a woman to whom He will offer that exact same choice. How amazingly fitting this encounter is at this very location. This was abundantly clear to the Savior.

It was here that Jacob, the patriarch of the twelve tribes, bought a plot of ground, by faith, before the Jews had ever entered the promised land. Jacob believed God would keep His promise and give his descendants this land. So he bought his own burial site here and would leave instructions to have his body transferred from Egypt to this spot after the land had been occupied by the Jews. This was a spot that represented the power of faith in the word of God. Jesus knew His Bible. He knew all this.

Here, Jacob built a well for his flocks and the flocks of his sons. Here, an altar to God had been built after the central campaign of the conquest of Canaan. The law of God was written on that altar as a symbol that the law of God was now the law of the land. The kingdom of God would be established here. I repeat: Jesus knew all this, and here came a woman He would offer that kingdom. Can you not see the absolute perfect artistry of God in all this? Don't tell me your Father in heaven didn't see you coming from a long way off. He is the One that orchestrated every step of your salvation journey! For goodness' sake, thank Him!

The sixth hour is either noon by Jewish time or 6:00 PM by Roman time. Scholars are divided on this point. It seems more logical from the times given at the end of this gospel describing the crucifixion event that John is using Roman time: 6:00 PM would seem more logical as Jesus was really weary (v. 6). At least He would have been wearier at 6:00 PM than He would have been at noon!

The Woman

Apparently, the well wasn't being used at this time of day. Nobody was there when the woman came. There is significance to the fact that the woman showed up at 6:00 PM and alone. Typically, towns were built around wells or a water source because of the importance of water in this arid region. Most likely, there was a well in the town square of Sychar. It can be expected that she had been socially banned from using that well, so she was forced to come to this well.

This would indicate that the woman was somewhat of a social outcast. Certainly, the rest of the story supports this proposition. She was alone. Usually, women would go to the well in groups, for safety. She was coming to this well that was about a half mile from the city of Sychar. Water was usually drawn in the morning. This was not the time women drew water. Everything about this scene throws suspicion on this woman's character.

When the woman arrives, Jesus initiated the conversation:

7. *Jesus said to her, "Give Me a drink."*

8. *For His disciples had gone away into the city to buy food.*
9. *Therefore the Samaritan woman said to Him, "How is it that You, being a Jew, ask me for a drink since I am a Samaritan woman?" (For Jews have no dealings with Samaritans.)*

Bold and Awkward

The fact that Jesus would initiate a conversation would mean nothing to us. But Jesus was a Rabbi. Rabbis were instructed to never talk to women in public, not even to their own wives or sisters. Rabbinical law taught that it was better to burn the law than to give it to a woman. Women were deemed unable to understand the law. Verse 8 simply indicates that Jesus and the woman are alone at the well. When Jesus asked her to give Him a drink, she was clearly taken aback.

One would think that a normal response would be to just give Him a drink as He asked. As we will see, this woman was not afraid of men, even strange men or Jewish men. Since Jesus opened the conversation, she was curious as well as confused by Jesus's request. She was not confused about Him being thirsty, but confused about Him speaking to her and asking her for something. Now, don't misunderstand me here. Given the culture and the context, and the two of them being there alone, she probably thought this guy was hitting on her! And it wouldn't have been the first time some stranger hit on her. Jesus had just crossed a huge social barrier. Had she been a proper Jewish woman, she would have said nothing and simply given Him a drink. She knew all of this, and her mind was starting to whirl with the impropriety of the situation.

Jesus's request was simple and straightforward enough, but totally over the top socially and morally. In some sense, I think she liked Him immediately after He asked for water. She probably thought He must also have been someone like her, over the top socially and morally! And He was, but not like she was thinking. So, she questioned Him about the inappropriateness of His request.

The conversation continued:

10. *Jesus answered and said to her, "If you knew the gift of God, and who it is who says to you, 'Give Me a drink,' you would have asked Him, and He would have given you living water."*
11. *She said to Him, "Sir, You have nothing to draw with and the well is deep; where then do You get that living water?*
12. *"You are not greater than our father Jacob, are You, who gave us the well, and drank of it himself and his sons and his cattle?"*

Confusion

Jesus steered the conversation in a completely new direction. "What is the 'gift of God' this man is speaking of? Who is this man speaking to me?" These were the questions that came to her mind. Sitting on this side of history, we know what Jesus was talking about. In Mark 1:8 and in John 7:37–39, we know that the gift of God is the gift of the Holy Spirit, the Comforter, that Jesus would send after his ascension. Jesus here describes this "gift of God" as living water. He also reveals that He is the One that is able to give this gift.

Does the woman know what Jesus is talking about? Of course not. It is obvious in the woman's response that she misunderstood, which is no surprise. Even the brightest theological mind on the planet, Nicodemus, misunderstood Jesus about being born again. But she is genuinely entering the dialogue. If Jesus is talking about being physically thirsty, why didn't he bring something to draw water? Certainly, He didn't expect folks to be at every well to draw water for Him, did He? And this well was particularly deep, about sixty feet deep. Yet He had offered her "living water." Well (no pun intended), where was He going to get this water, especially when He had nothing to draw with? His offer didn't make a lot of sense.

The "living water" Jesus spoke of was in sharp contrast to the "well" water she had come to draw. She understood that living water described bubbling, running, clean, continuous spring water. This well held anything but clear, clean spring water. The water in this well was still, stagnate, and collected as in a cistern. The water in this well was completely dependent on rain soaking through the soil. It didn't tap into any aquifer or underground water supply. It often ran dry.

Yet he spoke with such confidence that He seemed to be implying some ability. "If she knew the gift of God," "If she knew who he was," she pondered. His comments seemed somewhat bold, to say the least. Certainly, he could not have been greater than Jacob who gave the well in the first place.

The Bluff

She decided to call His bluff, *"Certainly, you are not greater than our father Jacob, are you?"* There, she challenged His lofty claim. She called His bluff. Jesus was sitting on the edge of the well at this time, resting. Jacob had provided this well, and this well had been supplying water for decades. He claimed He could give some kind of better water, "living water." Who did He think He was anyway?

Jesus replied:

13. *Jesus answered and said to her, "Everyone who drinks of this water will thirst again;*
14. *but whoever drinks of the water that I will give him shall never thirst; but the water that I will give him will become in him a well of water springing up to eternal life."*

Jesus stated the obvious. *"Everyone who drinks of this water will thirst again."* Well, duh. That was true of any water from any well. All water can only quench thirst for a while. You have to keep coming back. Yet Jesus was suggesting that the water He was offering her was quite different from the water she came to draw. He was offering water that quenched thirst *forever*! That's pretty remarkable, if it was true. This living water would certainly save her a lot of time and a lot of embarrassment.

Second, His water would spring up within her. She wasn't sure what that meant, but it sounded exciting. And finally, this water would somehow provide eternal life. "What is He really talking about?" she wondered.

Jesus had shifted the concept of thirst. He was not talking about a temporary or temporal physical thirst but a deep-seated, internal thirst. That much was becoming clear to her. He was talking about the universal thirst to know who God is, the thirst to know how to relate to God and to know what God's purpose was in life. Her mind began to flood with a hundred questions. Why did His words seem to penetrate her heart? How did her life ever get into the mess in which she found herself? Where was she really headed in life? Is there a God that is really interested in her? And what was life really all about anyway?

Jesus was saying that the living water, that only He could provide, would become an eternal spring within her, meeting the deepest needs and longings of the human heart; that He could provide the answers to all these questions; that He had the answers to what eternal life was all about. The woman clearly understood that Jesus was talking about something that drives toward the deepest needs and longings of her heart.

The woman replied with great anticipation, but with a cloud of doubt:

15. *The woman said to Him, "Sir, give me this water, so I will not be thirsty nor come all the way here to draw."*
16. *He said to her, "Go, call your husband and come here."*
17. *The woman answered and said, "I have no husband." Jesus said to her, "You have correctly said, 'I have no husband';*
18. *for you have had five husbands, and the one whom you now have is not your husband; this you have said truly."*

"Well, mister, put your money where your mouth is. Give me this water," she replied. She was not exactly sure what kind of water

He was talking about, but if it would quench her natural thirst forever and she wouldn't have to keep coming to this well, that was good enough for her. And if, somehow, this living water met the deeper needs of her heart and soul, all the better.

It is interesting that she didn't just dismiss Jesus as some kind of quack for making such an offer. There had to be something about Jesus' offer that was compelling to her. She had a sense that He was genuine and was certainly not hitting on her. His tone was sobering and sincere. He seemed to be speaking with authority even though she may not have understood exactly what He was talking about. There was definitely a ring of truth about Him. He was clearly not a nut, and He clearly was not coming on to her. He was talking in riddles, so she decided to pursue this line of thought. "If you've got it, I'll take it."

The Opening

Jesus, at this point, realized that the woman's heart had begun to open. He knew she didn't really understand what He was offering her. What was of primary importance to Jesus was that she understood _who_ was offering it. If she really understood and accepted who He was, there would be no problem with her accepting His offer of eternal life.

If Jesus would have come out from the beginning and said, "Hi, I'm the Messiah. You know, the One your prophets have told you about that was to come. Well, I'm here, and if you believe in me, I'll fill you with the Holy Spirit." If He took that approach, she would have immediately dismissed Him as a fruitcake.

What Jesus did was to start with a felt need, water. From there He gracefully moved to the real need, living water. What has become crucial is not so much that she understands what living water is, but who it is that is offering it. Therefore, He now begins to gently open the door to who He is.

Jesus said to her, *"Go, call your husband, and come here."* John tells us in chapter 1 that Jesus was the light that comes into the world that enlightens every man. This woman does not yet understand what Jesus is talking about because the light has not yet shown in her dark heart. Jesus is offering "living water," but before she will ever be able to understand or receive that living water, she needs to face clearly and squarely her own sin problem. Let me say right up-front, her sin has nothing to do with sex.

We will pursue this further in the next chapter.

Application

The dynamic of this story is that every day of the Christian life is designed by God as a "divine appointment." God does not lay out for any of us what our day ahead will reveal. Walking by faith is just that, a walk. One step at a time. We have no idea of whom or what we might encounter on any given day, but that's what makes our walk of faith so interesting. God is perfectly able, and often does turn an ordinary "chance meeting" into a divine appointment. Our responsibility is to be ready, to have our antenna up in anticipation of what God might be bringing our way. That is exactly why the Apostle Paul reminds young Titus to "be ready for every good deed."[124] Let God surprise you today with the opportunity for a good deed.

---

[124] Titus 3:1

CHAPTER 12

A Divine Appointment (Part 2)
John 4:19-42

I did! I got "taken in." I hate to admit it, but it's true. I was old enough; I should have known better. But I trusted the guy that offered me an opportunity to make a lot of money with almost no work. For a couple of hundred bucks, I could go to this seminar. At this seminar, I'd learn how to play the stock market and win every time. It wasn't illegal. The reason most people weren't doing this was because they didn't understand the stock market. So I paid my money and went to the seminar. I took the bait. If I could get rich by using my brain instead of my brawn, why not?

Wow. Talk about "hard sell!" For an additional $1,200 I could get the "starter set." I would be learning on my own, but it was supposed to be simple. For $4,000 I could get the elite set. That came with a 24/7 hotline service. I'd really get rich quick if I'd give them $4,000. If I waited until after the seminar was over, it would cost me $6,000. I could actually *save* $2,000 by spending $4,000 right now. The arguments were compelling. Long lines of men and women began to form to put down their money. What do I do? Am I passing up the opportunity of a lifetime?

Bottom line, I passed up my opportunity of a lifetime; and at this point in my life, I am so glad I did. WHAT A SCAM. I came so close to wasting $4,000 I'd never get back!

I wonder if this woman at the well wasn't having some of these same thoughts. Jesus was offering her living water. It sounded good. No, it sounded *great*. It could simplify her life so much by not having to come to this well almost every day. And she would be the envy of the town with her living water. But what was "living water?"

Before we go any further, let's get this concept of living water clear in our heads. Read carefully John's comment in John 7:37–39:

37. *Now on the last day, the great day of the feast, Jesus stood and cried out, saying, "If anyone is thirsty, let him come to Me and drink.*
38. *"He who believes in Me, as the Scripture said, 'From his innermost being will flow rivers of living water.'"*
39. *But this He spoke of the Spirit, whom those who believed in Him were to receive; for the Spirit was not yet given, because Jesus was not yet glorified.*

At the Feast of Tabernacles in the temple in Jerusalem, every day for six days the priest would bring a pitcher of water from the pool of Siloam and pour it into the silver basin by the altar of burnt offerings for sin. On the seventh day of the feast, the great day of the feast, this observance wasn't practiced. There was probably not one in a hundred Jews who observed this practice every year that knew what it symbolized. It had just become a routine part of the Feast of Tabernacles celebration. Most probably thought it had something to do with cleansing.

It was on that seven^th day of this feast, the great day, that Jesus stood up before the masses of worshippers, right at the moment in the celebration when the water would have normally been poured out, and shouted for all to hear, *"If any man is thirsty, let him come to me and drink. He who believes in Me, as the Scriptures said, 'From his innermost being shall flow rivers of living water.'"* In the next verse of the text John tells us, *"But this He spoke of the Spirit, whom those who believed in Him were to receive; for the Spirit was not yet given, because Jesus was not yet glorified."*

The priests themselves had long forgotten the significance of the symbolic act they were preforming. Here Jesus rings the bell loud and clear, reminding even the Jewish leadership of the significance of what they were doing and at the same time declaring who He was. The pouring out of the water at the altar was a picture of the pouring out of the Spirit that Jesus would send after His suffering and sacrifice as the Lamb of God. This is what was foreshadowed on that final, great day that had been celebrated annually for decades during the Feast of Tabernacles. He was the One with the authority to pour out the Spirit of God to any who believed in Him. What a spectacular scene that must have been! Can you imagine what Jesus's brothers must have thought, as they stood there and heard Him make this bold claim!

Both John and Jesus had been teaching that a cleansing of sin was necessary before anyone could receive the gift of living water, the filling of the Holy Spirit that Jesus offered. Before anyone can receive that gift of living water, they must first be cleansed through confession and repentance. That's why Jesus said, "Go call your husband." He was calling this lady to come face-to-face with her own personal sin.

True Confessions

The boldness of His request stunned her. Her mind raced. She felt exposed. Quick, she needed to hide. So, she threw a curve ball: *"I have no husband?"* It was the truth. "Where was He going with this?" she wondered.

Jesus had just touched a very sensitive nerve. This woman had been looking for love all her life, and she had never found it. Several times she had gotten excited about "falling in love." Each time she thought, "This is it" and that her deepest need for unconditional love would be fulfilled. Finally, there was someone who would love her for who she was. But every time, love eluded her. She had never found or experienced true, lasting, enduring love. She had never experienced a commitment that lasted through thick and thin. No one was ever willing to love her when she was unloveable. They had always abandoned her. And each time she sank deeper and deeper into despair.

Jesus told her that He knew she has had five husbands before and the one she was now with was not her husband. Many say, "There! There is a clear example of foreknowledge, a mark of His deity." I disagree that this was supernatural insight into this woman's life. This wasn't Jesus's first trip through Samaria. He had passed by this city many times before. For thirty years, at least three times a year and probably more, Jesus and his family walked down this road right past the city of Sychar. They probably often stopped at the same McDonald's Jesus had sent His men to.

It was a two-and-a-half-day walk from Cana of Galilee to Jerusalem. His parents were poor and couldn't afford the long four-and-a-half-day trip down to Jericho, across the Jordan, up the Jordan valley on the east to Bethany, across the Jordan again, and then up to Jerusalem. This route straight through Samaria was quicker, cheaper, and easier, and Sychar was a convenient halfway point to stop for the night.

What Jesus was saying to this woman was common knowledge. Everyone in Sychar knew that the woman was sleeping with a man to whom she was not married. Everyone knew she had been married five times previously. This woman was famous in an infamous way. Her reputation had preceded her. That is exactly why she is here at the well, all alone, at the wrong time of day.

She had never met Jesus before, but Jesus knew all about her. He had recently read a short article about her in the *Jerusalem Gazette* on page 4, beneath the fold, just a couple of days ago, as had all the other folks in town. The businessmen that traveled the area frequently talked about her. Her reputation has spread far and wide. The fact that she had been married five times before and was currently sleeping with a man she wasn't married to was common knowledge.

When she came to the well, Jesus realized why the Father *had* him go through Samaria. It was all too clear to Jesus that this was of the Father's making. It was a "divine appointment." Jesus had just touched her deepest need, the need for a deep and lasting love relationship that springs up from within. He had also touched her greatest area of weakness, her most shameful failure in life, her sin.

Her Interest Heightens

You would think with her personal life exposed to a total stranger, she would walk away. She doesn't:

19. *The woman said to Him, "Sir, I perceive that You are a prophet.*
20. *"Our fathers worshiped in this mountain, and you people say that in Jerusalem is the place where men ought to worship."*

At first glance, you would think this comment might be a deflection because of her embarrassment. I don't think so. There was something about the demeanor of Jesus that kept her engaged. We will see clearly what that "something" is when we get to chapter 16 of John's gospel. (It is the Father drawing her to Jesus.) We know from 3:17 that Jesus didn't come to judge, but to save. So, His comment about her situation did not have a condemnatory tone to it. She didn't feel Jesus was looking down on her. Besides, He had offered her "living water," whatever that was. From her reply, she sensed that Jesus was offering something deeper that just normal water. He was talking like a Rabbi would talk.

The question about the proper place to worship drove at the heart of her constant feelings of shame and guilt. She knew that He knew that she was really messed up. And for some inexplicable reason, she didn't feel judged or condemned by Him. It was as if she had been exposed in some way, but exposed to someone she could trust with deep secrets and her personal failures. She just didn't know how to get "unmessed up."

What was driving her was the need to be forgiven by God. But she didn't know how to get there. Her guilt was constantly before her. The folks in town wouldn't let her forget. Her belief, however, was that only by going to the temple could she find forgiveness. But where? What temple? And what if she couldn't get in? It was more complicated in her mind than it needed to be. So the question about where to find forgiveness, which temple, came out. It was a legitimate question and might get her pointed in the right direction.

The Jews and the Samaritans were really divided on the issue of the temple and worship. The Samaritan patriarchs said she needed to go to the temple on Mount Gerizim and find her forgiveness from God there. "You people," the Jews, said she must go to the temple in Jerusalem to find forgiveness from God there. She felt "damned if I do or damned if I don't" when it came to finding God's forgiveness and blessing. The woman is genuinely confused about the place and value of worship. She would really like to get out from under the guilt and shame she has lived with for almost her entire adult life.

True Worship

She realized now that Jesus must be some kind of prophet. In fact, He was probably a Jewish Rabbi or teacher. He seemed to know what He was talking about. She just needed to know how to find God and unload this burden she was carrying.

Jesus's response addressed directly what the woman as looking for: how to find God and the forgiveness she was seeking:

21. *Jesus said to her, "Woman, believe Me, an hour is coming when neither in this mountain nor in Jerusalem will you worship the Father.*
22. *"You worship what you do not know; we worship what we know, for salvation is from the Jews.*

23. *"But an hour is coming, and now is, when the true worshipers will worship the Father in spirit and truth; for such people the Father seeks to be His worshipers.*
24. *"God is spirit, and those who worship Him must worship in spirit and truth."*

Both the Jews and the Samaritans had it wrong. The Jews thought that God wanted to be worshiped in a temple made with stones and built in Jerusalem. The Samaritans thought that God wanted to be worshiped in a temple made with stones and built on Mount Gerizim. Both were wrong. The temple was never intended to be anything more than a symbol. The temple was designed, in all its complexity, as nothing more than a grand illustration.

The true temple in which God desired to be worshiped all along was a temple made without human hands. It was the temple of the human heart, made and formed by God. Worship was never intended to be an external exercise. That was also true of the law written on tablets of stones, which were also only a symbol of the law written on the tablets of human hearts, as Paul argues in 2 Corinthians 3:3. God desires to be worshiped in our inner man, in the human spirit. Since God is Spirit, He must be worshiped in spirit.

Truth has come, by divine design, through the Jews. Ultimately, truth is a person. Jesus said, *"I am the way, the truth and the life. No man comes to the Father but by Me."*[125] The very reason Jacob bought this land and dug this well was because he believed by faith the promises of God. He believed that God would be faithful to the promises He gave to Abraham and his descendants, the Jews. He believed that salvation would come from the Jews. And *now* is the time that God seeks those who will confess and repent for their sin and worship Him from their hearts. He seeks those who will "cast all their anxieties upon Him," and submit to His will for their lives.

---

[125] John 14:6

An Opportunity

In verse 24 Jesus offers this woman an opportunity to give her heart to the Lord. Any man, anywhere, at any time can chose to worship God in spirit and in truth. No temple required. Jesus is calling her to repent and receive from Him the "gift of God."

The woman replies

> 25. *The woman said to Him, "I know that Messiah is coming (He who is called Christ); when that One comes, He will declare all things to us."*

It is interesting that this Samaritan woman was waiting for and hoping in the same Messiah the Jews were anticipating. This reply tells us something about the ministry of John the Baptist. In Matthew 3:5, we learn that Jerusalem was going out to hear John, and all Judea and "all the district around the Jordan." Sychar was one of the "districts around the Jordan."

Because of the impact of John's ministry, all of Jerusalem, Judea, and all of the districts around the Jordan river were talking about the coming kingdom of God. The prospect of the coming of God's Messiah was on everyone's mind. This woman was filled with anticipation that a Messiah was coming, and she knows that Messiah will come from the Jews. Her hope was that when the Messiah came, He would finally answer the questions she had about how to find God and how to cast off her burden of guilt and shame. That is exactly what Jesus was referring to when He said "you worship that which you do not know; we worship that which we know." She knew that salvation would come through the Jews via a Messiah who had been promised. When that man comes, the Messiah, she will follow Him. Her faith is going to be in Him and only Him.

Here is the open door and Jesus takes full advantage of it:

> 26. *Jesus said to her, "I who speak to you am He."*

Her expression to this comment seemed to become frozen in time. Did she hear Him right? Did He just say that He was the Messiah? Could that really be possible? Then all of a sudden—bingo! The light came on. This made complete sense to Her. This was why He started the conversation and was talking to her. This answered all the questions she had regarding this man at the well. It must be true.

It is at this moment she believed who He was and what He was saying. Her heart screamed out to her to place her faith and trust in this man, Jesus. The conversation was over. She had heard enough. It now all made sense. Her heart was aching for that life-giving water, and she knew it had nothing to do with this silly well. The water she had just begun to taste, deep within her soul, was so much purer and sweeter than anything Jacob's well had ever offered. She had begun to drink of a well that was already beginning to bubble up within her unto eternal life, and that overflow of living water was about to be shared throughout the small town of Sychar. She was speechless, overwhelmed with joy. She was at a complete loss for words. If you notice in this text, John records no response from the woman to this mind-boggling statement by Jesus. Her gut reaction was to turn and run as fast as she could, back to town to tell everyone who she had just met.

For those who say that Jesus never claimed to be the Messiah, the promised Son of God that the Old Testament said was to come, here was the proof positive! He was telling her that He was the Messiah! Now the woman knew who she was talking to and knew that He could deliver on the living water He was offering her. She has become a believer.

A Simple Witness

Finally, the boys return with lunch (Jesus's sandwich, like mine, would have been the Big Mac with no onions!):

27. *At this point His disciples came, and they were amazed that He had been speaking with a woman, yet no one said, "What do You seek?" or, "Why do You speak with her?"*

28. *So the woman left her waterpot, and went into the city and said to the men,*
29. *"Come, see a man who told me all the things that I have done; this is not the Christ, is it?"*
30. *They went out of the city, and were coming to Him.*

When the disciples returned, they saw that Jesus was talking with the woman. It was clear to them that Jesus was stepping way over recognized social "taboos." Yet no one said anything. They had learned already that Jesus did things and said things that were a little "out of the box." This was another indication that they had been through Samaria before, for they knew good Jews didn't go this way to Galilee. They had come to realize that Jesus was a bit "unorthodox" in His ministry. Jesus never seemed to believe that "orthodoxy" was important.

This conversation with Jesus had three remarkable results. The first result in verses 28–29 was that the woman immediately began witnessing about the Messiah. She demonstrated exactly what witnessing was to be. She simply began telling others what had happened to her. Her comments weren't even theological. Her simple question was, *"This is not the Christ, is it?"* God doesn't ask you to be theologically accurate when you are talking about your experience with Him. All He asks is that you simply be genuine.

The woman's statement *"This is not the Christ, is it?"* did not mean that she doubted Jesus was what He said He was. She did not doubt that at all. She was looking for confirmation. Yet she was doing something very bold. She was addressing the *men* of the city.[126] This was a culture where women didn't address men in public, especially "loose" women. Yet she threw caution to the wind and addressed the men of the city who normally would have nothing to do with her publicly.

She soft sold "the Christ" with her question, because she knew few men would believe her. But she added to her credibility by freely

---

[126] John 4:28

admitting that He had told her *"all things that I have done."* She was no longer ashamed of what she had done. She had met the Christ, and He had accepted her with all her flaws! This woman knew what she had been, but now she knows she has been forgiven! That's what gave her courage.

The fact that she *"left her waterpot"* behind is interesting. What a fascinating illustration of a change in priority. She left behind that which was temporal and raced back to the city to share that which was eternal. Her invitation was so simple and direct: "Come and see the Man." That's what evangelism is all about. It is simply a testimony of your encounter with Jesus, coupled with the invitation, "Come and see the Man" for yourself. That was the very same invitation Jesus had given John and Andrew, the first disciples He recruited.

The effectiveness of this simple testimony was profound. God can use any clay pot, even one that is immoral and infamous. There were two things that must have captivated the attention of these towns-people. One was the great anticipation of the coming of the Messiah and the other was the obvious change in this woman after having met this strange man at the well. Again, the ministry of John the Baptist in the area, the notorious cleansing of the temple in Jerusalem, the stories of Jesus's miracles that had spread far and wide, and then this woman's encounter with One who claimed to be the very Messiah.

This was clearly the work of the Spirit of God. Her words fell with unusual power. They had never given her any account before; she was considered to be beneath them all. But now they were captivated because the Spirit of God was working through her.

Real Food

As the people of the city were coming out to the well (half mile from town), John describes a conversation Jesus was having with the disciples:

31. *Meanwhile the disciples were urging Him, saying, "Rabbi, eat."*

32. *But He said to them, "I have food to eat that you do not know about."*

33. *So the disciples were saying to one another, "No one brought Him anything to eat, did he?"*

The disciples realized Jesus was thirsty, hungry, and weary. So, they encouraged Him to eat. But this was a "teachable moment." Jesus saw a wide-open door. At the mention of food (which Jesus had completely forgotten about in this encounter with the woman), the contrast between physical food and spiritual food dawned on Jesus like a ton of bricks. Jesus pounced on the opportunity.

Jesus teased their thinking by saying He had food to eat that they knew nothing about. Of course, the disciples didn't understand what Jesus was talking about. They were thinking about physical food. Had someone else brought Him something to eat? But Jesus was not talking about physical food.

Do you see a pattern here? Jesus said to Nicodemus, "You must be born again." Nicodemus completely missed the point! Jesus said to the woman at the well, "I'll give you living water." The woman completely missed the point! Jesus said to His disciples, "I have food to eat you know nothing about." His disciples completely missed the point! You might argue, as I often have, "Why doesn't Jesus just speak plain *English*!? Why does He have to 'beat around the bush' so much?"

BUT NO! The real question is, why don't you get the wax out of your ears? Why don't you pay closer attention? Why don't you dig a little deeper?

This ought to give us some insight into studying the Bible. How often do we look at what is recorded in the Bible and completely miss the point God is making? I think this is why Bible study is boring for so many. They just don't dig deep enough. They don't ask enough questions of the text. They don't look under the rocks and behind the bushes. They don't put themselves in the sandals of the characters they are reading about. They don't see what's going on around the scene, hear the guttural sounds of the animals, smell the foul odors of the streets, feel the hot sand between their toes. They are just too lazy when they read the most important book ever given to humanity! It's more fun to read *Killing Jesus* by Bill O'Reilly than *Killing Jesus* by Pontius Pilot, which is directly inspired by God Himself! There is something wrong with this.

I don't believe everything in the Bible should be "spiritualized." I believe God's promises are literal. The Bible itself will reveal the rich treasures beneath the surface of scripture if we will just dig for them.

Jesus understood their confusion and defined exactly the food He was referring to:

> 34. *Jesus said to them, "My food is to do the will of Him who sent Me and to accomplish His work*

Did you notice that there were two parts to the food Jesus was referring to? First is to do the will of the Father that sent Him. That's why He has engaged this woman in conversation. It may have been in violation of cultural "norms," but it was the will of the Father. Second is to accomplish the Father's work. Simple; once you understand what the Father wants you to do, you do it. By following through with doing the Father's will, the desired result will be accomplished.

The Process

And the fruit of that accomplishment is about to land on them. Jesus sees it coming; the disciples do not. And herein lies another important spiritual point. Only if you are doing the Father's will can you perceive the accomplishments that the Father is bringing about. Far too many of us are too preoccupied looking down at our sandwich than we are looking out at the potential harvest. What is the Father's will in this particular situation? One might think it is to reach a desperate and lonely woman for Christ. But how shortsighted that is! God's will was to reach the entire town of Sychar, in Samaria, with the gospel message.

This is a very clear lesson that the disciples missed and one that I hope you see unfolding in John's gospel. In the book of Acts, the disciples, *after* the Holy Spirit (the gift of God) had fallen on them, *stayed* in a "holy huddle" in Jerusalem even though Jesus had commanded them to take the gospel to "Jerusalem, all Judea and Samaria and even to the uttermost parts of the earth."[127] It took the murder of Steven and the persecution of the church to squeeze them out of Jerusalem with the gospel message and get the movement going. Finally, Philip took the gospel to Samaria (this very place) at that time. These twelve could be very slow learners.

Jesus goes on to tell them how the divine process works:

35. *"Do you not say, 'There are yet four months, and then comes the harvest'? Behold, I say to you, lift up your eyes and look on the fields, that they are white for harvest.*

36. *"Already he who reaps is receiving wages and is gathering fruit for life eternal; so that he who sows and he who reaps may rejoice together.*

37. *"For in this case the saying is true, 'One sows and another reaps.'*

38. *"I sent you to reap that for which you have not labored; others have labored and you have entered into their labor."*

Jesus addresses a couple of important issues here. First, one of the problems we have with sharing our faith is in our thinking that we need to wait until the time is right before we say anything. The issue is never timing, it's one of perspective. This problem is described graphically in verse 35, *"Lift up your eyes."* We are continually looking "down" at the tasks immediately before us when we need to be looking "up" in anticipation of what God might be doing. "Lift up your eyes," Jesus exhorts them.

---

[127] Acts 1:8

The point is, we need to quit looking at our routine lives from the human, earthly point of view. We need to learn to begin to see our routine, daily life experiences, as opportunities to "do the will of God." We need to develop a divine, heavenly point of view. If we would just ask God for His perspective on the opportunities around us, we too would see that the fields are "white unto harvest."

Let me illustrate what I mean, because to be quite honest, I am just beginning to learn this (and I'm really *old*!). I have begun the practice of praying before every meeting, appointment, or activity every day. My prayer is simple and short: "Lord, let me see this next appoint from Your point of view and if there is an opportunity there, give me the grace to not pass it up. Give me the wisdom to accomplish Your will." Sounds simple, doesn't it.

Last week, I met with an associate over lunch to discuss a particular piece of property. This associate was not a believer and was a very experienced and successful businessman in his late fifties. We'll call him Bill. During lunch, after we had talked about this property, I said to him, "Bill, may I ask you a very personal question?"

His response was, "Sure, ask away."

So, I said, "What is your aversion to the faith?"

"Oh," he replied. "I don't have any aversion to the faith. I believe in God, I believe in Buddha, I believe in Judaism, I believe in Hinduism. I don't have any aversion."

I responded, "How come I didn't hear Christianity mentioned anywhere in your list?"

"That's easy," he said. "It's because Christianity is too narrow, too exclusive." And from there a beautiful conversation ensued about the faith. Clearly, God had opened a door. And I am grateful He gave me the courage and ability to walk through that door.

The second issue Jesus clarified here is that some sow, some reap, some gather. It's all part of one process. It is all part of what we call evangelism. Here is where so many Christians try to cop out of their duty to be a witness for Christ. How often have you heard someone (maybe yourself) say, "Oh, I don't share my faith openly. That's not what God has called me to do. My job is to sow seeds. My job is to do some watering. I never pick fruit."

Well, let me tell you something. If God puts a ripe peach that needs picking right in front of your face, I wouldn't want to be you if you try to tell God, "Gee, Lord, I just sow seeds. I can't pick this ripe peach in front of me." The truth is, we all do *all* these things when God puts them before us to do. We don't pick or choose if we are going to sow, water, or reap. We simply do what the Master requests at the moment.

None of us can ever take credit for any of it anyway. We all share, equally, often in ways we are not even aware. Another man's reaping may be our seed-planting and vice versa.

The Fruit

The disciples are about to share in the efforts of Jesus and the woman. They will begin sharing and baptizing many, many people—not because of their own testimony, but because of the efforts of Jesus and the testimony of the woman:

39. *From that city many of the Samaritans believed in Him because of the word of the woman who testified, "He told me all the things that I have done."*
40. *So when the Samaritans came to Jesus, they were asking Him to stay with them; and He stayed there two days.*
41. *Many more believed because of His word;*

Many believed in Jesus because of the woman, and many more believed because of Jesus's words. The woman and Jesus shared in the effort of reaching the Samaritans. The disciples also participated in baptizing them. Reaching people for Christ is *always* a team effort, and the team is called the church!

Notice how the growth of these new believers is expressed:

42. *And they were saying to the woman, "It is no longer because of what you said that we believe, for we have heard for ourselves and know that this One is indeed the Savior of the world."*

They began by believing what the woman said. Now, they believe because of Jesus's own teaching. What they believe is that Jesus was the Messiah, the Savior of the world. This was an amazing level of faith considering that almost none of the Jewish leadership in Jerusalem, that Jesus had spent so much time with at this point, had this level of faith. Nor were they willing to testify of Him to others, as this woman did.

One last issue we see here is that oftentimes, the most unexpected situations reveal the most productive results when it comes to divine impact. Those who were hated the most and despised the most are oftentimes the most open to accepting the gospel message.

All of us have family members or relatives that we think are so pagan they would never become Christians. Don't believe that for one second. Don't quit praying for them. Don't neglect opportunities to speak to them, regardless of how ineffective you feel it is. Remember, God's word is sharper than any two-edged sword.

Carol and I can testify to the fact that we have a son that we felt, at one time, we had completely lost to the enemy. But Carol (more than me) continued to pray and believe God for him. His "turnaround" was nothing short of miraculous. Today, I am meeting with him weekly, at his invitation, helping him understand the word of God in a weekly Bible study. There was a time not that long ago that I would never have believed this would be possible. God is still in the business of doing miracles.

Application

There are several concepts that most of us have thoughtlessly adopted that work against all that God has and desires for us. They are concepts like *routine, typical, impossible, normal, socially acceptable,* and *politically correct.* It has taken a very long time, but I have come to the conclusion that every moment of every day is an opportunity for God to interject something dynamic and supernatural into my experience. It's all a matter of prayerful expectation—keeping our focus "up" in anticipation, instead of "down," looking at the mundane. We'll never meet our own "woman at the well" if we are not willing to "step out of the box" on a moment's notice. Pray this week that God would give you the desire and courage to live one day in prayerful anticipation. Then when the door opens, just step through it.

CHAPTER 13

A Father's Faith
John 4:43-54

"Going home" seems like such a comforting, warm, and fuzzy feeling kind of a thought. It is a place of family, friends, and good memories; a place of safety, security, and acceptance. "Home" is about mom's cooking, sitting on the porch with dad, having your own room. It's a "safe" place.

But that may not always be the case. What if "home" wasn't such a fun, warm, and fuzzy place? What if home was a place of criticism, rejection, and scorn? What if those closest to you, your own family, thought you were just a little proud, arrogant, and "off balance" a bit? What if your siblings were jealous of you and the people in your own home town thought you were conceited, presumptive, and full of yourself? Those kinds of attitudes toward you would make going "home" somewhat awkward, to say the least. Yet that is exactly what Jesus faced as He headed back to Galilee with His men. Things hadn't exactly gone well the last time He was home, in Nazareth.

Jesus had tarried two days in Sychar at the urging of the towns-people. Indeed, the fields had been white unto harvest. What an amazing time they must have had there. The hospitality was over the top. I am sure the minds of Jesus's disciples were completely blown away. How could they have misunderstood and misjudged these Samaritan so harshly? What seemed so impossible just a couple of days earlier had bloomed into something they could never have imagined. They would never again look at Samaritans in the same way. Would that all of us would learn to see others through the eyes of faith instead of with eyes of prejudice, suspicion, and doubt. But now, it was time to continue on to Galilee.

In 4:43–45, John describes the awkwardness Jesus faced in Galilee:

43. *And after the two days He went forth from there into Galilee.*
44. *For Jesus Himself testified that a prophet has no honor in his own country.*
45. *So when He came to Galilee, the Galileans received Him, having seen all the things that He did in Jerusalem at the feast; for they themselves also went to the feast.*

In directing Jesus to return to Galilee, the Father had Him go through Samaria, the shortest route, for the reasons we observed in the last two chapters. (Galilee was a large region in the northern part of Palestine, about two thousand square miles in size. That's about the size of Snohomish County, here in Washington State.) He was heading home to familiar territory. His hometown was Nazareth of Galilee.

An Ominous Note

John opens with an ominous note in verse 44. Jesus Himself recognized that He was not given any respect in His hometown of Nazareth.[128] The event Jesus was referring to in verse 44 is recorded in Luke 4. He was recalling a time earlier in His ministry when had been given the opportunity to read the scriptures during the synagogue service in Nazareth. He read a passage out of Isaiah 61 that

---

[128] Mark 6:4

spoke about the Spirit of the Lord coming upon the Messiah and that the Messiah would be anointed to preach the gospel to the poor, proclaim release to the captives, restore sight to the blind, set free the downtrodden, and proclaim the favorable year of the Lord.[129] When he finished reading that text, He rolled up the scroll, laid it down, and made the statement, *"Today this Scripture has been fulfilled in your hearing."*[130]

Nobody missed the point. It was outrageous. Jesus was saying *He* was the one that scripture was taking about, *He* was the Messiah who was to accomplish all those things, *He* was the One that text was referring to! The folks in the synagogue that day in Nazareth didn't take that so kindly. They were filled with rage at His arrogance and presumption. In anger, they rose up as one, dragged Him out of the synagogue and out of town with the intent to kill. Blaspheme was a capital offense. They knew who He was. He was no Messiah. He was the carpenter's son. But He avoided their murderous intent by simply walking through their midst and leaving town. Some would argue, "There, you see. Jesus used His divine power to simply walk through the angry crowd unharmed" No! I don't see that. What I see is that the Father told Jesus to just walk away and it was the Father that restrained everyone. It was obvious however, from that point on, Jesus wasn't likely to be voted "the most likely to succeed" in Nazareth. They didn't much care for Him. Even His "own household" thought He had gone too far.[131]

One gets the feeling from John's statement in verse 44 that returning to Galilee wasn't something that Jesus looked forward to a great deal. It's hard for anyone to return to an area where you were not respected. It would seem that the rebuke He received of being only a carpenter's son from Nazareth had spread far beyond that small village of Nazareth into the whole region of Galilee.

---

[129] Luke 4:18–19
[130] Luke 4:21
[131] Matthew 13:57

A New Reputation

However, when Jesus returned to Galilee this time, there was an unexpected surprise. John tells us that the Galileans received Him. They openly and warmly welcomed Him home. John tells us why. They had seen what He had done in Jerusalem. Jesus had clearly established Himself as a respectable Rabbi in Jerusalem. The comment is interesting that they welcome Him because they had seen *"all the things that He did* in Jerusalem."

There were many from Galilee that had been at the feast in Jerusalem. They recognized Him as the man that had "cleansed the temple." The religious elite may have been angered, but the common folks saw that act as true religious zeal. Everyone knew the money changing at the temple was a scam. Jesus did what any number of them would like to have done if they could. They felt He was standing up for them. Many of the Galileans who had gone to Jerusalem for the Passover had believed in Him there because of the many signs He had been done.[132] It seemed that He had overcome the stigma the folks of Nazareth tried to pin on Him as just being "the carpenter's son."

Coming into the region, Jesus headed for Cana of Galilee:

46. *He came therefore again to Cana of Galilee where He had made the water wine. And there was a certain royal official, whose son was sick at Capernaum.*
47. *When he heard that Jesus had come out of Judea into Galilee, he went to Him, and was requesting Him to come down and heal his son; for he was at the point of death.*

John tells us the reason Jesus went to Cana and not Nazareth was because it was in Cana He had done His first miracle of turning water to wine. It was also the home of Nathaniel,[133] who most likely

---

[132] John 2:23
[133] John 21:2

provided them with a roof over their heads and comfortable lodging. Jesus went to Cana because it was there that the seeds of faith had been planted through that first miracle. This time, because the reputation of His ministry in Jerusalem preceded Him, He returned to a much wider and more accepting audience.

Cana was only two miles from Nazareth and Jesus knew that the primary motivation for His acceptance in the area was because of the miracles He had been doing in Jerusalem. It wasn't long before a royal official from Capernaum sought Him out. (Capernaum was about eighteen to twenty miles to the east of Cana, situated on the north end of the Sea of Galilee.) Upon hearing the news that Jesus had returned from Judea, the royal official saddled up and rode the eighteen miles to Cana to find Jesus.

A Desperate Love

The term *royal official* means one belonging to a king. This man was an official of the court of Herod; a Gentile in the service of the Roman government. The reason for his haste to see Jesus was because his son was sick. The term he used, "my little boy," was a term of endearment and tenderness. It showed the love and the anguish of this father for his son.

We are told that the boy's condition was very severe. He was *"at the point of death."* The official's son was dying, and there was nothing that could be done to save him. There is no question, because of the man's position as a member of the king's house, everything humanly possible to help his son had already been done with no success of any kind. Every doctor, psychic, and wizard in the area had been called to help. The boy's condition had been determined to be hopeless, and death was inevitable.

It was out of desperation that the father rode as hard as he could, pushing his mount to the limit to get to Cana. There was only one hope. It was a long shot, a *very* long shot, but if he could convince the miracle worker to come to Capernaum, his son just might have a chance. He had heard the rumors pouring back out of Jerusalem about the wonders this man Jesus had done there, healing all kinds of sickness. He had no idea if they were true or just exaggerations. But it didn't matter. All his other options had been exhausted. Jesus was his only hope.

I can clearly remember lying in a bed at Hogue Memorial Hospital in Newport Beach, California in 1960, at seventeen years of age, the night before they were to do exploratory surgery and remove at least three ribs on my right side because of a rare form of cancer. At my parent's insistence upon knowing, the specialist doing the surgery told us the chances of a successful surgery were less than 50 percent, but there were no other options.

I pleaded with God that night that if He would spare me, I would live for Him the rest of my life. I've often thought back on that promise, that I haven't been the best at keeping, why it is that we have to become so desperate *before* we seek God seriously? Why do we need to be broken before we can get fixed? I think, partially, it is because when we are broken, we realize we are not really in control of our own lives. And if there is no God that can help us, we are truly lost and hopeless. That is exactly how this father felt.

Upon finding Jesus, the royal official made two requests of Him: first, to come to Capernaum, and second, to heal his son. The verb tense *requesting* in verse 47 indicates a repeated action over time. He wasn't just asking Jesus to come to Capernaum and heal his son. He was begging Jesus, over and over again. This man was desperate because of the desperate love he had for his son.

What an interesting twist of fate. Here was a father who was in anguish because of his son who was about to die. He cried out to Jesus to save his son, and because of this father's love for his son, Jesus saved him. Our Father in heaven also had a Son who, Himself, was at the point of death, only death on a cross. Yet because of His great love for you and me, He allowed His only son to die a horrible death that you and I might be saved.

Is it not amazing that the Father, who could have saved his Son, forsook Him and allowed Him to die because He loved you and me so much? You could say, He loved you and me more than His own Son. That is a truly remarkable love. Jesus's identification with this man's anguish at the impending loss of his son must have been beyond description!

Jesus responded to this royal official:

48. *Jesus therefore said to him, "Unless you people see signs and wonders, you simply will not believe."*
49. *The royal official said to Him, "Sir, come down before my child dies."*

My goodness, what a harsh statement! It sounds like He is berating this poor man. Berated or not, the man insists that Jesus come before it's too late. It's important to see exactly who Jesus was addressing here. The statement in verse 48 indicates the plural. Jesus is addressing a class of persons, "all you people" (plural), not just this grieving father. This official was a "king's man," a nobleman. He was a member of Herod's retinue and thus a part of the governing class of Galileans. It was to this class of ruling elite that Jesus addressed His statement. He was speaking to those in positions of leadership among us.

These are those who have the attitude toward Jesus of "prove it before I will believe." They won't believe simply on the basis of His word, truth or not. They want proof. These are the "seeing is believing" types among us. "Unless God meets my demands and proves Himself to me, I'm not going to believe" is their attitude. When we get to the end of our study in John, you will meet another man who held this attitude. His name was Thomas, "Doubting Thomas," and he was one of the twelve.

Is There Faith Here?

Do you think this official has faith that Jesus can heal his son? That's not an easy question to answer. He had a lot of wishing and hope, but I'm not sure he had a full bucket of faith. For one thing, he certainly believed that Jesus couldn't do anything until he first came to Capernaum. Once He got there, He would probably have to lay hands on his son or hold him or say some words over him or do something to make the sickness go away. That is why it was imperative that Jesus come to Capernaum with him.

And that's just the point Jesus was making. This official wanted Jesus to *do something* in order to heal the boy. Jesus was trying to elevate this man's faith. Jesus didn't what the father to just believe in *what* He could do, but in *Who* He was. Jesus was seeking to draw him into a deeper quality of faith.

Real faith doesn't require *anything* to be done! It just requires trust, expecting the unexpected. Jesus didn't need to physically *do* anything. He didn't need to go to Capernaum. He didn't need to lay hands on the boy. He didn't need to pray over him. He didn't even need to say a word and, in fact, He didn't do any of these things—just like the "water to wine" miracle illustrated so powerfully. All Jesus said to the waiter at the wedding in Cana was, *"Draw some out now, and take it to the headwaiter."* He didn't say, "WATER, turn to wine," or mutter anything. He didn't even *need* to speak a word. He just did it. And He could just do it here with this man's son. Can you believe in Him without requiring Him to give you some "sign"? That's what Jesus is driving at.

This healing of the royal official's son is set in sharp contrast to the healing of the Centurion's son in Matthew 8:5–13. Read that passage and see the parallels and contrasts. Both were from Capernaum, both were officials, both had someone close to them in grave sickness, both sought out Jesus to heal their loved one.

However, the contrast is great. The royal official here repeatedly requested Jesus to come. The centurion in Matthew's account didn't want Jesus to be bothered with coming, even when Jesus offered to come. Unlike this official who thought Jesus needed to come in order to heal his son, that centurion *knew* Jesus could heal his friend with just a word. The faith from that centurion wrung from the lips of

Jesus, *"Truly I say to you, I have not found such great faith with anyone in Israel."*[134] That's the level of faith Jesus was trying to bring this royal official.

The thing that frustrated Jesus with the type of people this official represented was their unwillingness to take Jesus at His word. Just believing in His word wasn't enough for them. They thought He needed to "come and do." But He doesn't need to come and do anything. Jesus wants us to simply lay our requests before Him and trust Him for the outcome, whatever that may be. He does not want us to beg Him for this or that to make our lives better. Even the "wind and the waves" obey His very command. Faith is believing He will do what is best for us if we simply leave our requests with Him and not demand or require this or that outcome? This is a contrast between a faith that is real and a faith that needs "props."

Look what happens next:

50. *Jesus said to him, "Go your way; your son lives." The man believed the word that Jesus spoke to him, and he started off.*
51. *And as he was now going down, his slaves met him, saying that his son was living.*
52. *So he inquired of them the hour when he began to get better. They said therefore to him, "Yesterday at the seventh hour the fever left him."*
53. *So the father knew that it was at that hour in which Jesus said to him, "Your son lives"; and he himself believed, and his whole household.*
54. *This is again a second sign that Jesus performed, when He had come out of Judea into Galilee.*

From the text, can you discern the point at which faith became alive and real in this man's heart? That is a pretty tricky question and one for God alone to know with certainty. However, for my money,

---

[134] Matthew 8:10

it seemed to occur in verse 50 when Jesus said, *"Go your way; your son lives."* The text tells us the man "believed *the word* that Jesus spoke." Now, there's a pretty good definition of *faith*, "Believing the word of Jesus." It was at this point the man placed his faith in Jesus's word. It would take several more hours before his faith in Jesus would be confirmed.

The man's action that demonstrated his faith is revealed in the key statement, he *"started off."* He turned and headed home. He didn't bother Jesus any longer. "Started off" was the point where this royal official put his faith into action. He left Jesus, banking on the fact that what Jesus said was true. He had *"the conviction of things not seen."*[135] That's the definition of real, genuine faith.

Don't pass up the tremendous "chance" this man took by believing in Jesus's word. You would think that once you put your trust in Jesus, all your worries and concerns would automatically fade away. But in the real world, it doesn't always happen like that. Just because you trust Jesus doesn't mean that the enemy is not going to play with your mind, seeking to cause you to doubt.

He had come in haste with every intent of not returning to Capernaum without Jesus. Here he was now, going home without Him. As he mounted his horse and rode home, he was feeling an immense amount of pressure. What if he got home and the boy was still sick unto death? What if the boy died shortly after he arrived home? His wife would be devastated. He would be devastated. He would have kicked himself for the rest of his life that he did not put more pressure on Jesus to come back with him. He would have gone to his own death believing it was his fault that his son died.

I am sure this man was thinking just like every one of us would be thinking as he rode toward Capernaum and home. "Jesus said my son 'lives.' What does *live* really mean. Is he going to be alive, but brain dead? Will he live but the quality of his life be so poor that he would have been better off dying? If I would have just

---

[135] Hebrews 11:1

pressed Jesus a little longer, I might have persuaded Him to come. Am I blowing this?!" There is no question that both fear and new hope were mixing wildly in his mind and heart as his horse trotted the beaten path toward Capernaum while the sun slowly sank in the western sky.

The fact that he left is significant. That is faith in action, even in the face of doubt and confusion. This is faith—doing what God says even when it doesn't make sense. This is faith—believing when we don't and can't understand it. Real faith is believing and obeying *despite* all our doubts and uncertainties. That is what this man demonstrates. This is the faith that is illustrated throughout the scriptures.

This was the faith of Joshua who marched his army once a day around the city of Jericho and seven times on the seventh day. I'm sure everyone was wondering what they were doing and why. It was because of Gideon's faith in God that he surrounded an army of 135,000 Midianite swordsmen with only 300 men holding pitchers, torches, and trumpets. Wow, that must have felt ridiculous. These men had no clue what God was going to do, but it was what God had told them to do; and by faith, they were willing to do what everyone else intuitively thought was ridiculous.

Down in verses 52 and 53, the man's faith is confirmed. That is exactly why he is so interested in the "timing" of his son's healing. I'm sure when Jesus said, "Your son lives" the man glanced down at his watch. It was exactly the seventh hour, about 7:00 PM. When his servants told him that the fever left his son at 7:00 PM, there was not a single shred of doubt left in this man's mind any longer. Jesus was everything He claimed to be. His faith was now in who Jesus *was* and not just what Jesus could do. His faith was confirmed.

There is an interesting side note to this official that many scholars believe is true. Some believe this official is mentioned by name in Acts 13:1. In Acts 13, a great awakening of faith broke out in the church at Antioch that eventually changed the focus of the church from Jerusalem to Antioch.

In 13:1, five different prophets and teachers from Antioch are named including Saul (Paul), Barnabas, and a man named Manaen "who had been brought up with Herod the tetrarch." Manaen is mentioned nowhere else in the scriptures except Acts 13:1. "Brought up with" is one Greek word *syntrophos* meaning "a fellow nursling." It was a term used to describe an adopted child. This adopted child of Herod would have been a "king's man," a royal official of the court. There is no absolute certainty here, but it does make some logical sense that this is the same man we find here in John's gospel.

This is the first Gentile in John's gospel that we know of that has come to believe that Jesus is the Messiah. The message of deliverance and salvation reaches across all racial, religious, and political lines. It is a gospel that meets the one common need of every man, woman, and child; the need to be born again of the Spirit of God. It is a rebirth of soul, mind, and heart that addresses the deepest needs and longings of any man or woman.

John tells us in verse 54 that this is the second sign Jesus did when He came out of Judea into Galilee. With His first sign, turning water to wine, Jesus demonstrated why the Word became flesh and dwelt among us. The whole purpose of the incarnation was to take that which was ordinary (symbolized by water) and turn it into something extraordinary (symbolized by wine). It was God's intention in sending His only Son, to take an ordinary pot of stone and place within it a treasure of unspeakable worth. That is the miracle of what happens when, by faith, we believe in and receive the Messiah, Jesus.

With this second sign that Jesus preformed, the healing of the official's son, we see the overwhelming, transforming power of faith that is not limited to time or space. The point of this second sign is summed up in the words of verse 50, "HE BELIEVED THE WORD THAT JESUS SPOKE...AND STARTED OFF." When there was no tangible, physical evidence to prove anything, when all logic and reason cried otherwise, this man took God at his word and acted on it. That's faith in action. And that's a faith that is not bound by time or space. That is the faith that the Messiah seeks from all who believe in His name.

Application

Taking God at His word, without conditions, is really quite difficult. We are "hard-wired" to want to see "results" or "evidence" or "proof." Probably one of the most difficult truths to take by faith is Paul's statement in Romans 8:28, *"And we know that God causes all things to work together for good to those who love God, to those who are called according to His purpose."* That's a great word of encouragement to give to a friend who's going through a really tough time, but it's a horrible piece of advice to receive if you are the one going through a really tough time. "I've lost my job," "My wife's leaving me," "My kids hate me," "I just got the news that my cancer is terminal," "My child just died." How can these possibly work to *any good?*

Here's the test of real faith in all of these. The next time something hits you broadside, *big* or small, simply pray a prayer something like this,

> Lord, I don't understand what's happening, and it makes no sense to me, but I do understand a couple of things about You. I understand that You love me and that You will not forsake me. I understand that You always have my best interest at heart. Because of that, I am eternally grateful. I know You've called me to accept this difficulty that I don't understand. So now, Lord, I ask for the sufficient grace that You promised, to get me through this in a way that will bring glory to You.

About the Author

Husband of Carol. Father of Mandy, Ashley, Kip, and Lance. Grandpa to Riley, Ethan (whom the Lord took home with cystic fibrosis), Kady, Zoe, Berkeley and Cayden.

Graduated from Newport Harbor High School in Newport Beach, California, in 1961, from Orange Coast College in 1963, and from San Jose State University in 1967.

Having been raised in a Christian church as a child, it wasn't until I ran into the ministry of Campus Crusade for Christ as a college student that I learned that I could have a real, personal relationship with Jesus. However, real growth began as a Christian when I moved from the beach area of Southern California to San Jose and start attending Peninsula Bible Church and sat under the teaching of Ray Stedman. Ray made the Bible come alive, and I was hooked!

After graduating from college, I accepted a two-year internship at PBC under the mentorship of Dave Roper, one of the pastors. David threw me to the wolves for two years on the Stanford University camps as part of Stanford United Ministries and was relentlessly available to catch me when I fell. Through the influence of both Ray and Dave as a fresh college graduate, I learned to fall in love with the Word of God. Their modeling and teaching changed me forever. The Bible turned from being a boring chore to read into a life-changing, exciting discovery and adventure.

After that life-changing internship, I spent ten years as the college/high school pastor of South Hills Community Church in San Jose, California. Following that, I served five years as the teaching pastor of Redlands Bible Church. Then the Lord led me to Spokane, Washington, to start a new church, Inland Community Bible Church, where I was the teaching pastor for five years until we merged with Central Valley Bible Church to become Valley Bible Church.

After leaving professional ministry, I have spent the last twenty-five years as a realtor in the Spokane, Washington, and Coeur d'Alene, Idaho, area. I am currently a managing broker/co-owner of Live Real Estate in Spokane Valley, Washington.

My extracurricular passion is fly-fishing. If I fail to answer my phone, the likelihood is that I'm waist-deep on one of the many gin-clear trout streams here in the northwest. There is nothing more relaxing and mind-clearing than a four-weight Winston with a floating line and a personally tied elk hair caddis with rubbery legs freely drifting over the drop-off of a deep pool. That can get your adrenaline up in a hurry. Join me some time. I'd love to share the experience.

CPSIA information can be obtained
at www.ICGtesting.com
Printed in the USA
LVHW020901170619
621442LV00002B/405

9 781641 914772